YOKAI

Japanese Mysterious Monsters and Phenomena

伊藤慎吾［監修］
ITO Shingo［Supervisor］

ナツメ社

ブックデザイン	池田香奈子
DTP	長谷川慎一
イラスト	さきゅう
日文執筆	元井朋子
日文校正	夢の本棚社
英文翻訳	山本航
英文チェック	ジョン・ダッシュバック
英文校正	寺田祐二(Maple Tree English Plaza)
編集協力	市瀬恵(株式会社スリーシーズン)
編集担当	横山美穂(ナツメ出版企画株式会社)

Author ITO, Shingo

A professor at Hirosaki Gakuin University. Specializes in research on Japanese yokai culture, including narrative literature and character culture. He is the founder of the *Irui no Kai* (The Gathering of Other Beings), a group dedicated to reporting research, providing information, and engaging in discussions about non-human characters. His published works include "'What If?' Encyclopedia: How to Keep a Dragon" (Jitsugyo no Nihon Sha), "Minakata Kumagusu and Japanese Literature" (Bensei Publishing), and "A Literary History of Personification and Wars Between Different Species" (Miyai Shoten).

Book Design	IKEDA, Kanako
DTP	HASEGAWA, Shinichi
Illustration	Sakyu
Japanese Author	MOTOI, Tomoko
Japanese Proofreader	Yume no Hondanasha Co., Ltd.
English Translator	YAMAMOTO, Wataru
English Checker	DASCHBACH, John
English Proofreader	TERADA, Yuji (Maple Tree English Plaza)
Associate Editor	ICHINOSE, Megumi (Three Season Co., Ltd.)
Editor	YOKOYAMA, Miho (Natsume Shuppan Kikaku Co., Ltd.)

YOKAI
Japanese Mysterious Monsters and Phenomena
First Edition May 2025

Publisher
Natsumesha Co., Ltd.
Natsume Bldg. 1F 1-52 Kanda-Jimbocho, Chiyoda-ku, Tokyo, Japan 101-0051

Production
Natsume Shuppan Kikaku Co., Ltd.

Printing
Lan Printing Co., Ltd.

We will replace the book if it has a manufacturing defect.
No part of this book may be reproduced in any form beyond the limits set forth by copyright law without written permission from the publisher.
ISBN978-4-8163-7715-0 ©NATSUMESHA

目次 Contents

Part		
1	鬼の姿 *Oni* Forms	6
2	幽霊・怨霊 Ghosts and Vengeful Spirits	30
3	人の姿 Human Forms	52
4	獣の姿 Beast Forms	78
5	鳥・虫・魚などの姿 Birds, Insects, Fish, and Other Creatures' Forms	102
6	物の姿 Object Forms	124
7	さまざまな姿 Various Forms	146
8	現代の妖怪 Modern Yokai	166

コラム
Column

酒呑童子ゆかりの山々	Mountains Associated with *Shuten Dōji*	12
百鬼夜行絵巻	Picture Scroll of the *Hyakki Yakō*	20
鬼退治の英雄	Heroes Who Slayed *Oni*	28
怨霊とたたかう僧	A Monk Fighting Vengeful Spirits	35
怨霊も神になる日本	Japan, Where Vengeful Spirits Can Become Gods	40
幽霊の足	Ghosts Without Feet	51
家の中にいる神様	Household Gods	72
神隠しと通り魔	Spirit Abductions and Random Attackers	76
人に化ける獣	Shape-shifting Animals That Transform into Humans	85
安倍晴明	*Abe no Seimei*	94
予言獣	*Yogenjū* (Prophetic Beasts)	101
ツチノコ	*Tsuchinoko*	109
いろいろな龍	Various *Ryū*	122
付喪神絵巻	Picture Scroll of the *Tsukumogami*	128
日本のエクスキャリバー	Japan's Excalibur	138
鳥山石燕の妖怪画	*Toriyama Sekien*'s Yokai Art	145
地獄にちなむ土地	Places Associated with Hell	156
学校の七不思議	The Seven Mysteries of the School	176
都市伝説	Urban Legends	182
妖怪のミイラ	Yokai Mummies	187

この本に出てきた妖怪の主な伝承地
The Major Legendary Regions Where the Yokai in This Book Appeared　188

Part 1

鬼の姿
Oni Forms

鬼は角やキバがある悪魔のような化け物です。人を食べたり悪さをしたりします。
Oni are demon-like monsters with horns and fangs. They eat humans and cause mischief.

8
酒呑童子
Shuten Dōji

10
茨木童子
Ibaraki Dōji

13
悪路王
Akuro-ō

⑭ 天邪鬼
Amanojaku

⑮ 前鬼・後鬼
Zenki and Goki

⑯ 百々目鬼
Dodomeki

⑰ 夜行さん
Yagyō-san

⑱ 百鬼夜行
Hyakki Yakō

㉒ 家鳴り
Yanari

㉓ 餓鬼
Gaki

㉔ 鬼女紅葉
Kijo-Momiji

㉖ 鈴鹿御前
Suzuka-gozen

㉗ 安達ヶ原の鬼婆
The *Oni-baba* of Adachigahara

酒呑童子

[*Shuten Dōji* (Drunk *Oni*)]

昔は美男子だった大酒飲みの鬼の頭領です。
A heavy-drinking leader of the *oni* who was once a handsome man.

京都の大江山(おおえやま)に暮らしていた鬼で、赤く大きな姿で描かれています。茨木童子などの多くの手下とともに、人々をさらいました。作戦とは気付かずに、武術に優れた源頼光(みなもとのらいこう)(P28-29)とその臣下を迎え入れた結果、毒の入った酒を飲まされ寝込んだところを殺されますが、首だけになっても頼光の兜に噛みついたと伝えられています。この物語は多くの絵巻物に登場します。

Shuten Dōji was an *oni* who lived in Mount Ōe near Kyoto Prefecture and is depicted as large and red in appearance. Alongside many underlings, including *Ibaraki Dōji*, he abducted people. Unaware of a plot, he welcomed *Minamoto no Raikō* (pp. 28-29), a master of martial arts, and his retainers. As a result, he was tricked into drinking poisoned *sake*, fell asleep, and was killed. However, it is said that even after being decapitated, his severed head bit into *Raikō*'s helmet. This story appears in many picture scrolls.

茨木童子

[*Ibaraki Dōji*]

酒呑童子の相棒で、血の味を覚えて鬼に変化しました。
A companion of *Shuten Dōji*, who transformed into an *oni* after acquiring a taste for blood.

Part
1

Oni Forms

もともとは人間でしたが、生まれたときから歯や髪が生え揃い、親から恐れられて捨てられました。若い頃に偶然血の味を覚えたことで、巨体の鬼に変化して酒呑童子の配下になったとも伝えられています。源頼光の襲撃の際、渡辺綱に腕を切られ、後日、綱の伯母に化けて腕を取り戻しにくる話が有名で、謡曲や歌舞伎、浮世絵、小説、マンガなどの題材になっています。

Originally a human, *Ibaraki Dōji* was born with a full set of teeth and hair, which frightened his parents and led to his abandonment. It is said that in his youth, he accidentally tasted blood, which caused him to transform into a giant *oni* and became a subordinate of *Shuten Dōji*. A well-known story involves *Ibaraki Dōji* having his arm cut off by *Watanabe no Tsuna* during *Minamoto no Raikō*'s raid. Later, *Ibaraki Dōji* disguised himself as *Tsuna*'s aunt to retrieve the severed arm. This tale has been featured in *noh* plays, *kabuki*, *ukiyo-e*, novels, and *manga*.

COLUMN

酒吞童子ゆかりの山々

Mountains Associated with *Shuten Dōji*

酒吞童子にまつわる伝説は大江山以外にもあります。酒吞童子の出生地として、伊吹山（滋賀と岐阜の県境）が中世から知られており、また、新潟の国上山の国上寺も酒吞童子ゆかりの寺として古くから知られています。いずれも酒吞童子の生まれてから大江山に居住するまでの経緯を描く絵巻物が残っています。

Legends surrounding *Shuten Dōji* are not limited to Mount Ōe. Mount Ibuki, located on the border of Shiga and Gifu Prefectures, has been known as *Shuten Dōji*'s birthplace since the medieval period. Additionally, Kokujō-ji Temple on Mount Kugami in Niigata Prefecture, is also renowned as a site connected to *Shuten Dōji*. Picture scrolls detailing his birth and the events leading to his residence on Mount Ōe remain in existence at both locations.

悪路王

[*Akuro-ō* (Evil Road King)]

人々を怖がらせた東北の鬼のリーダーです。

A leader of *oni* in the Tōhoku Region who frightened people.

岩手の達谷窟に砦を構え、鬼たちを従えて悪事をはたらいた鬼で、東北地方に伝説が多くあります。東北へ勢力を広げに行った坂上田村麻呂に倒されたという説が有名で、古代大和朝廷に逆らった野蛮な賊の頭領がモデルといわれています。

Akuro-ō was a *oni* who established a fortress in the Takkoku no iwaya of Iwate Prefecture, leading other *oni* to commit evil deeds. Many legends about him exist in the Tōhoku Region. The most famous story is that he was defeated by *Sakanoue no Tamuramaro* when the latter expanded his influence into Tōhoku Region. It is said that *Akuro-ō* was modeled after the barbaric leader of a band of rebels who opposed the ancient Yamato court.

天邪鬼

[*Amanojaku* (Contrarian *Oni*)]

人の煩悩を象徴するひねくれ者の小鬼です。

A mischievous little *oni* who symbolizes human vices and stubbornness.

人の心を読み、わざと逆らっていたずらをする妖怪で、小鬼のような姿をしています。四天王などの仏像に踏みつけられている小鬼を指すことも。語源は『古事記』『日本書紀』に登場する「天探女」で、「天の邪魔をする鬼」という意味です。

Amanojaku is a yokai who reads people's minds and deliberately opposes them to cause mischief, often depicted in the form of a small *oni*. It can also refer to the small *oni* being trampled underfoot in statues of the Four Heavenly Kings. The term originates from the "*Amanosagume*" mentioned in the *Kojiki* and *Nihon Shoki*, meaning "an *oni* who hinders the heavens."

前鬼・後鬼

[*Zenki* and *Goki*]

人の子どもをさらっていた鬼の夫婦です。

A married *oni* couple who abducted human children.

奈良東部の深山に住む夫婦が死んだ子どもの肉を食べた後、生きながらにして鬼となりました。しかし、役行者(修験道の開祖)を信じて崇めるようになり、山岳修行者を守る鬼になりました。その子孫が今もいるそうです。

Zenki and *Goki* were a married couple living in a deep mountain of eastern Nara Prefecture. After eating flesh of a dead child, they transformed into *oni* while still alive. However, they came to revere *En no Gyōja*, the founder of *Shugendō* (mountain ascetic practices), and became protectors of mountain ascetics. It is said that their descendants still exist today.

百々目鬼

[*Dodomeki* (**Hundred-Eyed** *Oni*)]

100個の目が腕についた不気味な泥棒鬼です。
A sinister thieving *oni* with 100 eyes on its arms.

100匹の鬼の頭目でしたが、武将の藤原秀郷（ふじわらのひでさと）に退治されました。400年後に女性の姿で現れ、栃木の本願寺（ほんがんじ）で僧の説法を聴いて改心し、角を折って爪を寺に納めました。今でも寺には爪と鬼の姿絵が伝わっています。

Dodomeki was the leader of 100 *oni* but was defeated by a samurai *Fujiwara no Hidesato*. Four hundred years later, it reappeared in the form of a woman and, after listening to a monk's sermon at Hongan-ji Temple in Tochigi Prefecture, repented. The *oni* broke off its horns and offered its claws to the temple. To this day, the temple preserves the claws and a depiction of the *oni*'s form.

夜行さん

[*Yagyō-san* (Night Wanderer)]

節分や百鬼夜行の夜に首なし馬で徘徊する鬼です。
An *oni* who roams on a headless horse during *Setsubun* or the night of the *Hyakki Yakō*.

首なしの馬に乗って歩き回る一つ目の鬼です。出会うと投げられたり蹴り殺されたりするので、草履を頭に乗せて地に伏せると助かるといわれています。夜行さんに食事のおかずの話をすると、毛の生えた手を差し出します。

Yagyō-san is a one-eyed *oni* who rides a headless horse, wandering through the night. Encountering with him are dangerous, as he may throw or kick people to death. It is said that placing straw sandals on your head and lying face down can save you. If you talk about side dishes with *Yagyō-san*, he will extend a hairy hand.

百鬼夜行

[*Hyakki Yakō*]

出会ったら死ぬ、化け物たちの真夜中の行進です。
A midnight procession of 100 monsters that brings death to anyone who encounters it.

Part **1** *Oni* Forms

鬼や妖怪などの化け物たちが、深夜に群れて歩く様子のことで、百鬼夜行に出会うと死んでしまうといわれています。出没する日が1〜2月は子の日、3〜4月は午の日などと毎月決まっていたため、人々はその日の外出を控えたほどでした。京都の一条通の大将軍商店街では妖怪仮装行列や妖怪フリーマーケット「モノノケ市」が行われています。

Hyakki Yakō refers to a parade of *oni*, yokai, and other supernatural creatures roaming together late at night. It is said that encountering the procession results in death. Specific days for its appearances were fixed by month—such as the Rat Day in January and February, and the Horse Day in March and April—leading people to avoid going out on those days. In Kyoto Prefecture, Ichijō Street this procession, and events like the Yokai Costume Parade and the "*Mononoke* Market", a flea market, are held in the Taishōgun Shopping District to celebrate this tradition.

COLUMN

百鬼夜行絵巻

Picture Scroll of the *Hyakki Yakō*

紙を横に長く繋いだ巻物に絵を描いた「絵巻物」にも妖怪が描かれています。15 〜 16 世紀に鬼や物の姿をした妖怪が行進している『百鬼夜行絵巻』が描かれると、今日までに多くの模本が制作され、その後の妖怪のイメージに大きな影響を与えました。それらの多くは道具箱の中から現れて、あたりを行進し、太陽とともに消えていくという構成になっています。なかでも大徳寺真珠庵にある、室町時代の絵師の土佐光信によって描かれたものが最も有名です。

Yokai also appear in *emaki*, or picture scrolls, which are long, horizontally connected pieces of paper painted with illustrations. During the 15th-16th crntury, the *Hyakki Yagyō Emaki*, depicting a procession of *oni* and yokai in the forms of objects and creatures, was created. Many reproductions have been made over the years, and these scrolls greatly influenced the depiction and imagination of yokai that followed. Most of these scrolls depict the yokai emerging from within toolboxes, parading around, and disappearing with the sunrise. Among them, the most famous is the housed at Daitoku-ji Templs's Shinjuan painted by the Muromachi-era artist *Tosa Mitsunobu.*

出典:国立国会図書館「イメージバンク」

家鳴り

[*Yanari* (House Rattle)]

家に潜む小鬼たちで、日本版ポルターガイストです。
Small *oni* who hide in houses, similar to a Japanese version of poltergeists.

地震でもないのに家が揺れたり、きしんで音を出したりすることを、昔から「家鳴り」と呼んで妖怪の仕業と考えてきました。江戸時代に作られた妖怪画集『画図百鬼夜行』には、小鬼が縁の下や柱を揺らして家鳴りを起こす様子が描かれています。
Unexplained creaking, shaking, or sounds in a house not caused by earthquakes have long been called "*Yanari*" and were attributed to the work of yokai. An art collection of Edo-era, *Gazu Hyakki Yakō* depicts small *oni* shaking the pillars or crawling under the floorboards to create these disturbances.

餓鬼

[*Gaki* (Hungry Ghost)]

仏教の教えが由来の鬼で、主に餓死者がなります。
A type of *oni* derived from Buddhist teachings, primarily those who died from starvation.

山中を歩く人などに取り憑いて歩けなくします。もともと旅先で餓死したり、不慮の事故で死んだりして成仏できない霊が人に憑くといわれています。米粒を道端に置いたり、おにぎりを放ったりして供養すれば、動けるようになります。

Gaki are said to haunt travelers, causing them to become unable to walk. These spirits are believed to originate from those who died from starvation while traveling or from unexpected accidents, leaving them unable to pass on peacefully. It is said that offering grains of rice by the roadside or throwing rice balls as an act of memorial can appease them, allowing the afflicted person to move.

鬼女紅葉

[*Kijo-Momiji*]

わが子のために鬼になった女性の物語です。
The story of a woman who became an *oni* for the sake of her child.

多くの鬼が住むことで有名な長野の戸隠山の鬼女です。美女だった紅葉は都で源経基の寵愛を受けましたが、えん罪で戸隠に追放されました。そのときにお腹にいた子を育て、「父に会わせてやりたい」と考えた紅葉は、資金を貯めるために鬼女となって人々を襲うように。その後、息子とともに倒されますが、今も鬼がいない里「鬼無里」として地名が残っています。

Kijo-Momiji is a female *oni* from Mount Togakushi in Nagano Prefecture, a place famous for its association with many *oni*. *Momiji* was once a beautiful woman who was favored by *Minamoto no Tsunemoto* in the capital. However, she was falsely accused of a crime and exiled to Togakushi. There, she raised the child she was pregnant with at the time and, wishing to reunite the child with his father, became an *oni* to accumulate wealth by attacking people. Eventually, she was defeated along with her son. The area is still known as *Kinasa* (the village without *oni*), preserving her story in its name.

鈴鹿御前

[*Suzuka-gozen*]

ヒーローと恋に落ちて、子をなした鬼女です。

A female *oni* who fell in love with a hero and bore his child.

三重と滋賀の県境にある鈴鹿山に住んだとされる鬼女です。女盗賊だった鈴鹿御前を成敗しにきた坂上田村麻呂と恋に落ちました。鈴鹿御前は自分の罪を悔いて鬼退治を助けたという話や、鈴鹿御前は天女や女神だったという説があります。

Suzuka-gozen is said to have been a female *oni* residing in Mount Suzuka, on the border between Mie and Shiga Prefectures. She was a bandit leader who fell in love with *Sakanoue no Tamuramaro*, the warrior sent to subdue her. Some stories say that *Suzuka-gozen* repented for her crimes and aided in slaying other *oni*. There are also versions of the tale where she is portrayed as a celestial maiden or goddess rather than an *oni*.

安達ヶ原の鬼婆

[The *Oni-baba* of Adachigahara]

旅人を迎え入れて殺害し、その肉を食べる鬼婆です。
An *oni* hag who welcomes travelers into her home, kills them, and eats their flesh.

旅の僧が福島の安達ヶ原で一晩の宿を借りるべく一軒の民家を訪れると、一人暮らしの老婆に快く迎えられました。老婆に見るなと言われた部屋を僧が覗くと、人骨の山があり、僧は逃げ出しました。観音の力で鬼婆は退治されました。

A traveling monk visited a solitary house in Adachigahara, Fukushima Prefecture, seeking shelter for the night. The elderly woman living there welcomed him warmly but warned him not to look into a certain room. The monk's curiosity got the better of him, and when he peeked inside, he discovered a pile of human bones. Terrified, he fled, and with the divine power of *Kannon*, the *Oni-baba* was defeated.

COLUMN

鬼退治の英雄

Heroes Who Slayed *Oni*

鬼退治で最も有名なのは、平安時代中期の貴族で武士の源頼光(みなもとのらいこう)(946〜1021年)です。酒呑童子(P8-9)や土蜘蛛(P110-111)をはじめ、数々の鬼や化け物を退治したという伝説が残っています。ほかにも、地獄にいる鬼を倒したという人物が2人います。天狗(P54-55)に武術や剣術を学んだ源義経(みなもとのよしつね)(1159〜1189年)は、父親を捜して地獄にいき、襲ってきた鬼を返り討ちにしました。朝比奈三郎(あさひなさぶろう)(1176〜?年)は地獄へ落とそうとする閻魔(えんま)(冥界の王で、死者の生前の罪を裁く神)のことを叩きのめして極楽へ案内させました。

The most famous figure in *oni*-slaying legends is *Minamoto no Raikō*, a nobleman and warrior from the mid-Heian-era (946–1021). He is renowned for defeating *Shuten Dōji* (pp. 8–9), the *Tsuchigumo* (pp. 110–111), and many other *oni* and monsters. Two other figures are known for battling *oni* in the underworld. *Minamoto no Yoshitsune* (1159–1189), who learned martial arts and swordsmanship from *Tengu* (pp. 54–55), ventured into the underworld to search for his father and defeated attacking *oni*. *Asahina Saburō* (1176–?) is said to have beaten *Enma* (the King of the Underworld who judges the sins of the dead) when the god tried to cast him into hell, forcing *Enma* to guide him to paradise instead.

Part 2

幽霊・怨霊
Ghosts and Vengeful Spirits

昔から「草木も眠る丑三つ時(午前2時～2時半)」に幽霊が出やすいといいます。
It has long been said that ghosts are more likely to appear during the "Dead of Night" (2:00 to 2:30 a.m.), when even the grass and trees are asleep.

32
お岩
Oiwa

34
お菊
Okiku

36
菅原道真
Sugawara no Michizane

38
平将門
Taira no Masakado

39
崇徳院
Sutoku-in

42
橋姫
Hashihime

44
産女
Ubume

45
七人ミサキ
Shichinin Misaki

46
生霊
Ikiryō

48
船幽霊
Funayūrei

50
大首
Ōkubi

31

お岩

Oiwa

日本で最も有名な女幽霊です。
The most famous female ghost in Japan.

江戸時代の歌舞伎『東海道四谷怪談』(1825年初演)に代表される「四谷怪談」は、日本で最も有名な怪談です。お岩の家に婿入りした浪人・民谷伊右衛門は愛人が妊娠したため、邪魔になったお岩に毒を飲ませて醜い姿にして家を乗っ取ります。裏切られたお岩は怨霊となって伊右衛門ほか関係者を祟っていきました。お岩を祀る於岩稲荷田宮神社が東京の四谷にあります。

The story of *Yotsuya Kaidan*, first performed in the *kabuki* play *Tōkaidō Yotsuya Kaidan* in 1825, is the most famous ghost tale in Japan. *Oiwa* married the *rōnin Iemon Tamiya*, who, after impregnating his mistress, poisoned *Oiwa* to disfigure her and took over her house. Betrayed and wronged, *Oiwa* became a vengeful spirit, cursing *Iemon* and others involved. *Oiwa* is enshrined at Oiwa Inari Tamiya Shrine in Yotsuya, Tokyo.

お菊

[*Okiku*]

井戸で皿を数えるエピソードが有名です。
Famous for the episode where she counts plates in a well.

屋敷で働いていたお菊が、10枚セットの皿を割ったと濡れ衣を着せられて井戸で亡くなり、その井戸から皿を数える声が聞こえるという怪異です。兵庫の姫路にはお菊を祀るお菊神社があります。

Okiku was a servant accused of breaking one of a set of ten plates, a crime she did not commit. She died tragically by the well, and her vengeful spirit is said to haunt the well, counting plates and lamenting. This eerie tale is one of Japan's most famous ghost stories. In Himeji, Hyogo Prefecture, *Okiku* is enshrined at the Okiku Shrine.

COLUMN

怨霊とたたかう僧
A Monk Fighting Vengeful Spirits

幽霊祓いに力を尽くした祐天(ゆうてん)(1637〜1718年)という僧侶がいました。なかでも有名なのが累という怨霊を祓う話です。累(るい)という醜い女は殺された兄とよく似ていたため「かさね」と呼ばれていました。累は夫にも疎まれて殺されてしまいます。その後、怨霊となってしまいますが、祐天によって祓われました。

There was a monk named *Yūten* (1637–1718) who devoted himself to exorcising ghosts. Among his most famous stories is the exorcism of the vengeful spirit *Kasane*. *Rui* was an ugly woman who was called "Kasane" because she closely resembled her murdered brother. *Rui* was despised by her husband and eventually killed by him. After her death, she became a vengeful spirit but was vanquished by *Yūten*.

菅原道真

[*Sugawara no Michizane*]

悲運の天才が怨霊になり、京都を騒然とさせました。
A tragic genius whose vengeful spirit caused chaos in Kyoto Prefecture.

若い頃から天才だった菅原道真は、とても早く出世しました。それが周囲から反感を買い、謀反の汚名を着せられて九州の太宰府に左遷されてしまいます。失意のうちに道真が亡くなると、道真を陥れた人が次々と死に、怪異が相次ぎました。道真の祟りだと大騒ぎになり、その魂を鎮めるために京都に北野天満宮が建立されました。福岡の太宰府天満宮には道真の遺骸が葬られています。

Sugawara no Michizane was a prodigy who rose quickly through the ranks of the imperial court, but his rapid success sparked resentment. Falsely accused of treason, he was exiled to Dazaifu in Kyūshū Region, where he died in despair. After his death, those who conspired against him began dying mysteriously, and strange phenomena plagued Kyoto Prefecture. Believed to be caused by *Michizane*'s vengeful spirit, the turmoil led to the establishment of Kitano Temmangū Shrine in Kyoto Prefecture to appease his soul. His remains are interred at Dazaifu Temmangū Shrine in Fukuoka Prefecture.

平将門

[*Taira no Masakado*]

切り落とされた首が強い怨念で空を飛びました。
His severed head, filled with strong resentment, flew through the sky.

自ら新天皇と名乗った平将門は、反逆者とみなされ打首になりました。その首は平安京にさらされた後、関東地方に向かって飛んでいきました。首塚や胴塚など将門にまつわる伝説は茨城や千葉を中心に関東地方周辺にたくさんあります。

Taira no Masakado declared himself the new emperor, which led to him being labeled a rebel and executed by beheading. After his head was displayed in Heian-kyō (modern Kyoto Prefecture), it is said to have flown to the Kantō Region. Many legends about *Masakado* are tied to the area, with numerous sites such as burial mounds for his head and body, particularly in Ibaraki and Chiba Prefectures.

崇徳院

[*Sutoku-in* (Emperor *Sutoku*)]

元天皇が我慢の限界を超えて怨霊になりました。

A former emperor who, having reached the limits of his endurance, became a vengeful spirit.

崇徳院は父の鳥羽上皇に疎まれ、天皇の位を奪われ、弟の支持派によって都も追われました。怒りのあまり怨霊と化し、天狗の首領となりました。その後、香川の白峰宮に祀られ、人々を守っています。

Emperor *Sutoku* was shunned by his father, Retired Emperor *Toba*, stripped of his throne, and driven out of the capital by supporters of his younger brother. Consumed by anger, he transformed into a vengeful spirit and became the leader of *tengu*. Later, he was enshrined at Shiramine Shrine in Kagawa Prefecture, where he is now worshipped as a protector of the people.

COLUMN

怨霊も神になる日本

Japan, Where Vengeful Spirits Can Become Gods

日本には御霊信仰という考えがあります。恨みを残して死んだ人の魂が、その恨みを晴らすために人々に悪さをしてしまうと怨霊になります。魂も感情をもっているとされていて、その怨霊が祓えないほど力が強い場合、神として祀ることで怒りを収めようとするのです。恐れながらも敬意を示しています。怨霊が御神体として祀られている神社は菅原道真（P36-37）の北野天満宮、平将門（P38）の神田明神などがあります。

In Japan, there exists a belief called *Goryō Shinkō* (spirit veneration), where vengeful spirits are enshrined as deities. When people die with lingering grudges, their souls can become vengeful spirits (*onryō*) that cause harm in an attempt to settle these grudges. Vengeful spirits who died senseless or tragic deaths often harbor such strong resentment that they cannot be exorcised, and they possess great power. By enshrining them as deities, people attempt to pacify their anger and redirect their power toward positive purposes. People respect them while feeling fear. Some shrines where vengeful spirits are enshrined as divine entities include Kitano Temmangū Shrine, dedicated to *Sugawara no Michizane* (pp. 36-37), and Kanda Myōjin, dedicated to *Taira no Masakado* (p. 38).

橋姫

[*Hashihime* (The Bridge Princess)]

神に願って鬼になった娘で、橋の守護神です。
The guardian deity of bridges, a girl who prayed to the gods to become an *oni*.

外敵から守る守護神として、大きな橋のたもとに祀られています。嫉妬に狂った公卿の娘が、「恨みを晴らすために鬼になりたい」と神社にこもりました。鬼となった後に、相手の男女やその縁者までもとり殺したため、鎮めるために橋姫として祀られました。京都の宇治橋(うじばし)の橋姫は嫉妬深さが特に有名で、婚礼の際は宇治橋を通らないようにしたともいわれます。

As a guardian deity protecting bridges from external enemies, *Hashihime* is enshrined at the base of large bridges. The story tells of a court noble's daughter, driven mad by jealousy, who secluded herself at a shrine, praying to become an *oni* to exact revenge. After transforming into an *oni*, she killed the man, woman, and even their relatives. To pacify her vengeful spirit, she was enshrined as *Hashihime*. The *Hashihime* of Uji Bridge in Kyoto Prefecture is particularly famous for her jealousy, and it is said that wedding processions would avoid crossing Uji Bridge, taking a detour instead.

産女

[*Ubume*]

日本の幽霊画と縁の深い、赤子を抱いた母の妖怪です。
A ghost who is a mother holding a baby. A yokai deeply connected to Japanese ghost paintings.

難産で亡くなった女性が妖怪になったもので、腰巻き姿で赤子を抱き、道ゆく人に「赤子を抱いてくれ」と迫ります。抱いた赤子がどんどん重くなったり、いつのまにか石に変わったり、赤子を抱いて不思議な力を授かることもあるのだとか。
A yokai formed from a woman who died in childbirth. She appears wearing only a loincloth, holding a baby, and begs passersby to "hold the baby." The baby grows increasingly heavier once held, sometimes turning into a stone, or, in some cases, granting mysterious powers to the person who holds it.

七人ミサキ

[*Shichinin Misaki* (The Seven Capes)]

水辺に７人で連れ立つ幽霊です。

A group of seven ghosts who appear together by the waterside.

海で亡くなった亡霊が７人連れ立って水辺に現れます。出会うと高熱を出して死ぬといわれ、１人加わると１人が成仏して常に７人組なのだそう。切腹を命じられた吉良親実の怨霊が、七人ミサキになったという高知の伝承が有名です。

The spirits of those who drowned in the sea appear as a group of seven by the waterside. It is said that encountering them causes a high fever and death. When one ghost joins the group, another finds peace and departs, ensuring the group always remains seven. Also, a famous legend from Kochi Prefecture tells of *Kira Chikazane*, who was ordered to commit *seppuku* whose vengeful spirits became the *Shichinin Misaki*.

生霊

[*Ikiryō* (Living Spirit)]

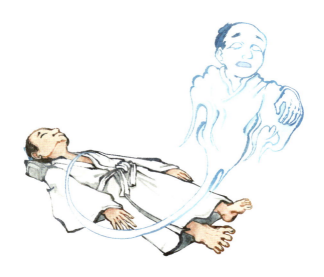

生きている人間の魂が無自覚に相手にとり憑きます。
The soul of a living person unconsciously possesses someone else.

Part **2** Ghosts and Vengeful Spirits

生きている人間の霊魂が体の外に出て恨みを晴らしたり、誰かにとり憑いたりします。死を前にした人が別の場所で目撃される、死の瞬間に親しかった人に会いに行くなどの生霊は各地で目撃されています。『源氏物語(ものがたり)』に登場する光源氏(ひかるげんじ)の愛人・六条御息所(ろくじょうのみやすんどころ)は生霊を飛ばし、妻の葵上(あおいのうえ)を死に追いやるという文学史上で最も有名な生霊です。

The soul of a living person leaves their body to exact revenge or possess someone. They have been witnessed in various forms, such as a dying person appearing in a different location or visiting loved ones. The most famous *ikiryō* in literary history is that of *Rokujo no Miyasundokoro* from "The Tale of Genji," who sent hers to torment and ultimately cause the death of *Genji*'s wife, *Aoi no Ue*.

船幽霊

[*Funayūrei* (Ship Ghosts)]

柄杓で船を沈没させるあの世からの使者です。
Messengers from the afterlife who sink ships using ladles.

日本各地の海に現れる怪異です。水難事故で死んだ人たちが現れ、あの世に引き入れようとします。「柄杓を貸せ」と言うことが多く、貸してしまうと船を沈没させられるため、海に出るときは底を抜いた柄杓を用意したといいます。船幽霊に出会ったら、おにぎりを海に投げ入れたり、火箸で船を撫でたりと、地域によって追い払う方法はさまざまです。

A supernatural phenomenon appearing in seas across Japan. *Funayūrei* are the spirits of those who died in drowning accidents and attempt to drag the living to the afterlife. They often ask, "Lend me a ladle," and if given one, they use it to sink the ship. To prevent this, sailors would prepare ladles with holes in the bottom. Methods to ward off *Funayūrei* vary by region, including throwing rice balls into the sea or stroking the ship with fire tongs.

大首

[*Ōkubi* (Giant Head)]

空を漂う巨大な首で、人を襲うことはありません。
A giant floating head in the sky that does not attack people.

2〜3mほどの大きな首が空中に現れ、人々を驚かせます。既婚女性の印であるお歯黒をした女性が多いことから、女性の怨念が妖怪になったもの、もしくはキツネなどが化けたものだとされています。江戸時代の随筆や怪談話に登場します。

A massive head, approximately 2-3 meters in size, appears in the air and startles people. Often depicted as women with blackened teeth—a sign of married women—it is believed to be the result of a female grudge turning into a yokai or a transformation by foxes or other creatures. It frequently appears in essays and ghost stories from the Edo-era.

COLUMN

幽霊の足

Ghosts Without Feet

日本では幽霊というと足がないものを思い浮かべる人が多くいます。これは江戸時代後期に京都で活躍した画家の円山応挙(まるやまおうきょ)(1733〜1795年)が描いた『返魂香之図(はんごんこうのず)』という足のない幽霊画が広まったことで、幽霊には足がないというイメージが定着したと考えられています。返魂香は死んだ人の魂を呼び戻すお香です。

In Japan, many people imagine ghosts as having no feet. This image is believed to have become fixed in the popular imagination after the widespread circulation of *Hangonkō no Zu* ("Portrait of Ghost with Return-Soul Incense"), a painting of a footless ghost by *Maruyama Ōkyo* (1733-1795), an artist who was active in Kyoto during the late Edo-era. *Hangonkō* was a type of incense believed to call back the souls of the dead.

Part 3

人の姿
Human Forms

人のような姿で人間にいたずらしたり、人間を助けたりする妖怪です。
They are yokai that take human form and either play tricks on humans or help them.

54
天狗
Tengu

58
だいだらぼっち
Daidarabotchi

60
ろくろ首
Rokurokubi

62
一つ目小僧
Hitotsume-kozō

63
子泣き爺
Konaki-jiji

64
のっぺらぼう
Noppera-bō

65
小豆洗い
Azuki Arai

66
山姥
Yama-uba

68
山童
Yamawaro

69
雪女
Yuki-onna

70
座敷童
Zashiki-warashi

74
二口女
Futakuchi-onna

75
ぬらりひょん
Nurarihyon

53

天狗

[*Tengu*]

赤い顔に高い鼻が有名な、山にすむ妖怪です。
A kind of mountain-dwelling yokai, the most famous being known for its red face and long nose.

天狗にはさまざまな種類がいますが、特に有名なのが赤い顔に高い鼻、大きな翼をもち、山伏の恰好をしている「鼻高天狗」です。山に住み、天災を起こしたり人をさらったりします。山で起こる不思議な出来事は天狗の仕業とされ、神とも妖怪とも考えられてきました。京都の愛宕山、鞍馬山、福岡と大分の県境の英彦山、東京の高尾山が天狗の山として有名です。

There are various types of *tengu*, but the most famous is *Hanataka Tengu*, characterized by its red face, long nose, large wings, and the attire of a *yamabushi* (mountain ascetic). *Tengu* dwell in the mountains, causing natural disasters or abducting people. Strange occurrences in the mountains were often attributed to the work of *tengu*, who had been regarded as both gods or yokai. Notable mountains associated with *tengu* include Mount Atago and Mount Kurama in Kyoto Prefecture, Mount Hiko on the border between Fukuoka and Oita Prefectures, and Mount Takao in Tokyo.

天狗いろいろ

Various Types of *Tengu*

鼻高天狗
[*Hanataka Tengu* (**Long-Nosed *Tengu***)]

身分の高い人や徳の高い僧が、生きながら、または死後、鼻高天狗になることがあります。

High-ranking individuals or virtuous monks may become *Hanataka Tengu* either during their lifetime or after their death.

烏天狗
[*Karasu Tengu* (**Crow *Tengu***)]

鳥のようなクチバシをもっています。武術や剣術に優れていて空を飛び回ります。

They have beak-like mouths resembling birds. Skilled in martial arts and swordsmanship, they fly freely through the sky.

八天狗
[*Hattengu* (The Eight *Tengu*)]

特に力が強い8人の鼻高天狗です。愛宕山の太郎坊（京都）、比良山の次郎坊（滋賀）、鞍馬山の僧正坊（京都）、飯縄山の三郎坊（長野）、大仙の伯耆坊（鳥取）、英彦山の豊前坊（福岡）、大峰山の普鬼坊（奈良）、白峰山の相模坊（香川）がいます。

Particularly powerful eight *Hanataka Tengu*. They include: *Tarōbō* of Mount Atago (Kyoto Prefecture), *Jirōbō* of Mount Hira (Shiga Prefecture), *Sōjōbō* of Mount Kurama (Kyoto Prefecture), *Saburōbō* of Mount Iizuna (Nagano Prefecture), *Hōkibō* of Mount Daisen (Tottori Prefecture), *Buzenbō* of Mount Hiko (Fukuoka Prefecture), *Bukkibō* of Mount Ōmine (Nara Prefecture), *Sagamibō* of Mount Shiramine (Kagawa Prefecture).

だいだらぼっち

[*Daidarabotchi* (The Giant of the Mountains)]

日本各地の地形を作ったとされる伝説の巨人です。
A legendary giant said to have shaped the terrain across various regions of Japan.

日本各地で語り継がれる伝説の巨人で、だいだらぼっちが山や湖を作ったという話が日本各地に残されています。例えば「山を作ろうとして掘ったところが琵琶湖になり、土を盛ったところが富士山になった」「富士山と重さ比べをしていた筑波山を落としたら男体山と女体山の２つになった」「足跡が湖になった」など、ダイナミックでスケールの大きな伝説とともに語り継がれています。

A legendary giant passed down in Japanese folklore, *Daidarabotchi* is said to have created mountains and lakes across Japan. Stories of *Daidarabotchi* can be found throughout the country, such as, "The area dug out to create a mountain became Lake Biwa, and the piled-up soil became Mount Fuji," "Mount Tsukuba split into two peaks, Mount Nantai and Mount Nyotai, during while he was comparing its weight with Mount Fuji," and "Footprints left by *Daidarabotchi* turned into lakes." These dynamic and grand-scale legends continue to be shared to this day.

ろくろ首

[*Rokurokubi* (Long-necked Ghost)]

伸びる首タイプと離れる首タイプ、2種類います。
There are two types: the stretching neck type and the detaching neck type.

首がひものように細く伸びるのものと、首が体から離れて自在に活動するものの2種類がいます。昼間は普通の人として生活し、寝ている間に首が抜けたり伸びたりすることが多いです。ほとんどが女性として描かれています。首に輪のような跡があるのは「ろくろ首」の印だと伝えられています。似たような妖怪は中国（飛頭蛮）や東南アジアでも記録されています。

There are two types: one whose neck stretches thin like a string, and another whose neck separates from the body and moves freely. During the day, they live as ordinary people, but at night, their necks often detach or stretch while they are sleeping. Most are depicted as women. It is said that a ring-like mark on the neck is the sign of a "*Rokurokubi*." Similar yokai have also been recorded in China (*Hitōban*, or "Flying Head Barbarians") and Southeast Asia.

一つ目小僧

[*Hitotsume-kozō* (One-Eyed Boy)]

目が1つだけしかない子どもの化け物です。
A child monster with only one eye.

日本ではとても有名な妖怪で、目が1つしかない子どもの姿をしています。人を驚かすだけで特に害はありません。静岡や関東地方では12月8日や2月8日に一つ目小僧がくるといわれ、驚かすため棒に刺した目の荒いザルをつるしました。

In Japan, it is a very famous yokai that takes the form of a child with only one eye. It poses no particular harm and merely surprises people. In Shizuoka Prefecture and the Kantō Region, it is said that the *hitotsume-kozō* appears on December 8 or February 8. To ward it off, people would hang a coarse sieve on a stick as a deterrent.

子泣き爺

[*Konaki-jijī* (Crybaby Old Man)]

赤ちゃんくらいの大きさのおじいさんの妖怪です。

A yokai appearing as an old man, but the size of a baby.

体は小さいものの、その姿はおじいさんそのもので、赤ちゃんのような泣き声で人を引き止めます。抱き上げると、体重が少しずつ重くなり、降ろそうとしても降ろせず、最後にはその人の命を奪うとされています。

Although its body is small, it has the appearance of an old man and stops people with a cry resembling that of a baby. When someone picks it up, its weight gradually increases, and no matter how hard they try, they cannot put it down. In the end, it is said to take the person's life.

のっぺらぼう

[*Noppera-bō* (Faceless Ghost)]

目鼻口のないのっぺりした顔で、人を驚かせます。

With a smooth, featureless face lacking eyes, nose, and mouth, it startles people.

姿は人間ですが、顔に目・鼻・口がありません。ある男が目鼻口のない女を見て驚いて逃げ、そば屋の主人にそれを話すと、「こんな顔だったかい?」と振り返った主人の顔ものっぺらぼうだったという話が有名です。

Its appearance is human, but its face has no eyes, nose, and mouth. A famous story tells of a man who, startled by a woman with a featureless face, ran away and recounted the encounter to a *soba* shop owner. The owner then turned to him and asked, "Was it a face like this?" revealing that he, too, was a *Noppera-bō*.

小豆洗い

[*Azuki Arai* (The *Azuki* Red Bean Washer)]

水辺に現れて、小豆を洗う音を立てます。
It appears by the water, making the sound of washing *azuki* beans.

日本全国で目撃されている妖怪で、川や井戸でシャカシャカと小豆を洗うような音を立てて人を怖がらせます。その正体はキツネやタヌキ、イタチといった動物、水死した老婆など、諸説あります。

A yokai witnessed across Japan. It creates a rustling sound as if washing *azuki* beans in rivers or wells, scaring people. Its true identity is subject to various theories, including animals such as foxes, *tanuki* (raccoon dogs), or weasels, or even the ghost of a drowned elderly woman.

山姥

[*Yama-uba* (Mountain Witch)]

山奥に住む老婆の妖怪で、人間を食べます。
A yokai in the form of an old woman living deep in the mountains, who eats humans.

山に入ってきた人を襲ってその肉を食べる恐ろしい存在として、古くから知られています。その一方で、山で出会った山姥を助けるとよいことが起きたり、仲良くなると農作業を手伝ってくれたりと、人を幸せにする存在でもあります。子どもを助けることもあり、クマと相撲をとるほど怪力な子ども・金太郎を育てたことは有名です。

Known since ancient times as a terrifying being that attacks people who enter the mountains and eats their flesh. However, on the other hand, if you help a *Yama-uba* you encounter in the mountains, good things may happen, or if you befriend her, she might assist with farming. She is also known to help children and famously raised *Kintarō*, a child so strong he could wrestle with bears.

山童

[*Yamawaro* (Mountain Child)]

山に住む子どもで、山仕事を手伝ってくれることも。
A childlike being who lives in the mountains and sometimes helps with mountain work.

山での仕事を手伝ってくれます。山童の通り道に建物を建てると悪いことが起こります。河童（P148-149）が山に住みついたものともいわれ、人と相撲を取ったり、いたずらしたりもします。

They assist with work in the mountains. However, if a building is constructed along a *Yamawaro's* path, bad things will happen. It is also said that *Yamawaro* are *Kappa* (pp. 148-149) who have settled in the mountains. They are known to wrestle with people and play pranks as well.

雪女

[*Yuki-onna* (Snow Woman)]

人を凍死させる、真っ白い衣装を着た女性です。
A woman dressed in pure white who causes people to freeze to death.

雪の降る夜に現れる白装束の女で、息を吹きかけられて凍死したり、生気を抜かれたりします。雪女に頼まれて赤子を抱くとその赤子が巨大になるなど、産女（P44）に似た話もあります。最も有名な雪女は東京の青梅に現れました。

A woman in white robes who appears on snowy nights, causing people to freeze to death with her breath or draining their life force. Similar to tales of *Ubume* (p. 44), there are stories where a *Yuki-onna* asks someone to hold a baby, only for the baby to grow enormous. The most famous *Yuki-onna* is said to have appeared in Ōme City, Tokyo.

座敷童

[*Zashiki-warashi*]

いれば繁栄し去れば衰退する、家に憑く子どもです。
A child spirit that attaches itself to a house, bringing prosperity while present and decline if it leaves.

家に住む子どもの精霊で、座敷童がいる家は栄え、反対にいなくなると衰退するといわれています。見た目は3〜10歳くらいの子どもで、おかっぱ頭で描かれることが多いです。パタパタと走る足音を立てたり、寝ている間に枕や布団を引っ張るいたずらをしたりします。福の神として大切にされており、食事や好物のものを供える人もいます。

A child spirit that resides in a house, it is said that a home with a *Zashiki-warashi* will prosper, while one without it will decline. Appearing as a child between 3 and 10 years old, it is often depicted with a bobbed haircut. *Zashiki-warashi* are known for playful mischief, such as making pattering footsteps or pulling pillows and blankets while people sleep. Revered as a deity of fortune, some people offer meals or the spirit's favorite items as offerings.

COLUMN

家の中にいる神様

Household Gods

日本にはたくさんの神様がいて、山や海などの自然をはじめ、すべてのものに神様が宿っていると考えられています。昔は家の中に神様を祀る祭壇(神棚)があったり、庭に祠があったり、お札を祀ったりしていました。それほど日本人は身近に神様を感じながら暮らしていました。

例えば家の中には、外から悪いものが入ってこないように玄関で見張る角大師（つのだいし）や蘇民将来（そみんしょうらい）、屋根の上には鐘馗（しょうき）、台所には三宝荒神（さんぼうこうじん）、トイレには厠神（かわやがみ）などがいます。

In Japan, it is believed that there are many gods and that they reside in everything, including nature, such as mountains and oceans. In the past, households often had *kamidana* (altars) for enshrining deities, small shrines in the yard, or *ofuda* (talismans) displayed, reflecting how closely Japanese people lived with the presence of gods.

For example, within the home, there are deities such as *Tsuno Daishi* and *Somin Shōrai* at the entrance to ward off evil, *Shōki* on the roof, *Sanpō Kōjin* in the kitchen, and *Kawayagami* in the toilet.

二口女

[*Futakuchi-onna*]

頭の後ろにもう1つの口がある女の妖怪です。

A female yokai who has another mouth on the back of her head.

後頭部にあるもう1つの口で大量のご飯を食べます。意地悪な継母が前妻の子を餓死させた後に後頭部に口ができたという話や、ケチな男の元に現れた飯を食わない女が実は二口女で、後頭部の口で大食いするという話があります。

She eats large amounts of food with the extra mouth on the back of her head. There are stories of a cruel stepmother who starved her stepchild to death and then developed a second mouth on the back of her head, and a woman who appeared not to eat in front of a stingy man but was actually a *Futakuchi-onna* who consumed large amounts of food with the mouth on the back of her head.

ぬらりひょん

[*Nurarihyon*]

坊主頭の老人か海の怪異で、つかみどころがありません。
Either a bald-headed old man or a sea creature, it's hard to determine.

江戸時代の絵画や文学の中に老人の姿で描かれますが、実態はよくわかっていません。岡山では頭くらいの大きさの丸い玉が海に浮いていて、取ろうとするとすりぬけ海底に沈んでは浮かび上がることを繰り返して人を驚かせるそうです。
While depicted as an elderly man in Edo-era paintings and literature, its true nature remains unclear. In Okayama Prefecture, it is said to appear as a round object about the size of a head floating in the ocean. When someone tries to grab it, it slips away, repeatedly sinking to the ocean floor and resurfacing to startle people.

COLUMN

神隠しと通り魔

Spirit Abductions and Random Attackers

ある日突然、人や子どもが姿を消すことを「神に連れ去られた」と考え、「神隠し」と呼ばれてきました。特に遊んでいる子どもが行方不明になることが多く、「天狗隠し」と呼ぶ地方もあります。

また、昔はぼんやりしていると「通り悪魔」に取り憑かれるといわれていました。姿は老人や武士などさまざまですが、それを見て慌てると悪いことが起こるため、心を落ち着けることが大切です。理由なく道行く人を襲う犯罪者を「通り魔」と呼びますが、「魔に憑かれた人の行為」と考えられていたからです。

When people or children suddenly disappeared, it has been believed they were "taken away by the gods" and called *Kamikakushi* (spirited away). This happens especially often to children while they are playing, and in some regions it is called *Tengu-kakushi* (taken by *Tengu*). Also, in the past, it was said that if you were absentminded, you could be possessed by a *Tōri Akuma* (passing demon). These demons could appear in various forms like elderly people or *samurai*, but it is important to remain calm when seeing them, as panicking would bring misfortune. The term *Tōrima* (random attacker) used today for criminals who attack random people on the street comes from the belief that such people were "possessed by demons."

Part 4

獣の姿
Beast Forms

キツネやタヌキ、犬、猫など、獣の姿をした妖怪です。
They are yokai in the form of animals such as foxes, *tanuki*, dogs, and cats.

化け狐

[*Bake-gitsune* (Shape-shifting Foxes)]

長生きをすればするほど、化ける力が増化します。
The longer they live, the more their ability to transform increases.

キツネは年を経ると妖力を得て人間を化かすようになります。九尾の狐（P82）のような大妖怪になるものもいますが、通常は人間にいたずらをする程度です。山道を歩く人を化かして道に迷わせたり、まんじゅうだと言って馬のフンを食べさせたり、温泉に入ったつもりで肥溜め（肥料にする糞尿を溜めておくところ）に入れたりしました。

As foxes age, they gain supernatural powers and begin to deceive humans. While some become great yokai like the *Kyūbi no Kitsune* (p. 82), most just play tricks on humans. They might have bewitched travelers on mountain paths to make them lose their way; tricked people into eating horse dung by making it look like *manjuu* buns; or fooled people into thinking they're entering a hot spring when it's actually a manure pit (where human and animal waste is collected for fertilizer).

九尾の狐

[*Kyūbi no Kitsune* (Nine-Tailed Fox)]

美女に化け、アジア各国で要人たちを騙し続けました。
Disguised as a beautiful woman, it had deceived prominent figures across various Asian countries for a long time.

古代インドで王子をそそのかして1000人もの首を切らせたり、中国で王妃になって2つの国を滅ぼしたりしました。その後、日本で玉藻前（P83）という女官に化けました。古くは尻尾が2本でしたが、江戸時代に9尾になりました。

In ancient India, it enticed a prince to behead a thousand people. In China, it became a queen and destroyed two nations. Later in Japan, it transformed into a court lady named *Tamamo-no-Mae* (p. 83). While originally depicted with two tails, during the Edo-era this changed to nine.

化け狐いろいろ

Various Types of Shape-shifting Foxes

玉藻前
[*Tamamo no Mae*]

那須（栃木）で退治され、殺生石となって今に残ります。石の毒気に当てられて、飛ぶ鳥は墜落し、周辺の動物は倒れるといわれます。

She was vanquished in Nasu (Tochigi Prefecture) and transformed into the *Sesshō-seki* (Killing Stone), which remains to this day. It is said that the toxic aura of the stone causes birds flying nearby to fall and animals passing through the area to collapse.

葛の葉
[*Kuzunoha*]

人に化けて安倍保名と夫婦になり、後に安倍晴明（P94）となる男子を産みました。

A fox who transformed into a human and married *Abe no Yasuna*, giving birth to a son who would later become *Abe no Seimei* (p. 94).

化け狸いろいろ

Various Types of Shape-shifting *Tanuki* (raccoon dogs)

化け狸
[Bake-danuki]

人に化けて、いたずらをするタヌキです。四国には化け狐よりも化け狸がたくさんいます。

These are *tanuki* that transform into humans to play tricks. There are thought to be more *Bake-danuki* than *Bake-gitsune* in Shikoku Region.

分福茶釜
[Bunbuku Chagama (The Lucky Teapot)]
群馬の茂林寺に伝わるタヌキが化けた茶釜で、いくら汲んでも湯が尽きないそうです。

A teapot at Morin-ji Temple in Gunma Prefecture that was a transformed *tanuki*. It is said that no matter how much hot water is drawn from it, it never runs dry.

COLUMN

人に化ける獣

Shape-shifting Animals That Transform into Humans

キツネやタヌキをはじめとして、ムジナや猫、カワウソなど、人に化ける動物がたくさんいます。人を驚かすだけの比較的無害なものもいれば、人を殺そうとする恐ろしいものまでさまざまです。不思議な現象や自然災害など、当時の科学では説明できないことを妖怪の仕業にしたのかもしれません。

There are many animals that can transform into humans, including foxes, *tanuki*, *mujina* (badgers), cats, and otters. Some are relatively harmless tricksters, while others try to kill humans to drink their blood. These yokai stories may have emerged as ways to explain mysterious phenomena and natural disasters that couldn't be explained by the science of the time.

犬神

[*Inugami*]

憑かれた人を不幸にする、飢えた犬の霊です。
A starving dog spirit that brings misfortune to those it possesses.

人を呪う際に使われた妖怪で、犬神に憑かれた人はさまざまな病気にかかったり、犬のような行動をしたりします。見た目はネズミのような小動物や、白黒の斑点模様のイタチのような動物、赤と黒の斑がある手のひらサイズの犬などといわれています。代々犬神を使役している「犬神持ち」の家系もあり、主人の考えを読み取って、主人の憎む相手にとり憑きます。

This is a yokai used to curse people. Those possessed by *Inugami* suffer from various illnesses or begin to behave like dogs. Its appearance is described variously as a small rodent-like creature, a weasel-like animal with black and white spots, or a palm-sized dog with red and black patches. There are also family lineages known as "*Inugami-mochi*" (*Inugami* handlers) who have inherited the ability to control these spirits for generations. The *Inugami* can read its master's thoughts and possesses those whom its master hates.

送り犬

[*Okuri-inu* (Escort Dog)]

人を守る「送り犬」と、人を襲う「迎え犬」がいます。
There are "escort dogs" that protect people and "ambush dogs" that attack them.

夜の山中などを歩いているときに後ろをついてきて、山賊やほかの獣から守ってくれるのが送り犬です。無事に目的地に着いたら、礼を伝えたり、握り飯などを渡したりすると帰っていきます。

The *Okuri-inu* follows people walking in the mountains at night, protecting them from bandits and other beasts. Once the person safely reaches their destination, the dog leave after receiving thanks or offerings such as rice balls.

猫又

[*Nekomata*]

年寄りの猫は尻尾が 2 股に分かれた猫又に変化します。
Elderly cats transform into *Nekomata* that have forked tails.

年を経て妖力を得た猫で、尻尾が 2 股に分かれていると考えられています。人や家畜を襲ったり、人に化けて悪さをしたりします。昔から猫は魔物と近いものと考えられてきました。山中に住む猫と飼い猫が猫又になる場合があります。

A *Nekomata* is a cat that has gained supernatural powers with age, and is typically believed to have a forked tail. They attack humans and livestock, and can transform into humans to cause mischief. Since ancient times, cats have been considered to be closely associated with supernatural beings. Wild mountain cats and domestic cats can transform into *Nekomata*.

鎌鼬

[*Kamaitachi* (Sickle Weasel)]

つむじ風に乗って現れ、大きな爪で人を傷つけます。
Kamaitachi appears riding whirlwinds and wounds people with its large claws.

つむじ風の中に身を隠し、人を切りつける妖怪です。気づかない間に刃物で傷つけられたような跡が残っているとき、「鎌鼬に切られた」などと言います。多くは大きな爪をもったイタチとして描かれます。切られたときは特に痛みがないものの、その後に大量出血し死に至ることもあります。鎌鼬は全国的に出現します。

This is a yokai that hides in whirlwinds and cuts people. When someone finds unexplained cuts on their body as if made by a blade, people say they "were cut by a *Kamaitachi*." It is often depicted as a weasel with large claws. At the moment people were cut, the cuts themselves are painless, they can lead to severe bleeding and sometimes death. The *Kamaitachi* appears throughout Japan.

すねこすり

[*Sune-kosuri* (Shin Rub Phantom)]

すねをこすって逃げる、犬のようなかわいい妖怪です。
A cute dog-like yokai that rubs its body against people's shins and runs away.

岡山に伝わる犬のような姿の妖怪で、雨の降る夜中に現れて、歩く人のすねをこすって通ったり、股の間をすり抜けたりします。歩いている人の足にまとわりつくため、人を転ばせることもあります。捕まえようとすると逃げ去ります。

A dog-like yokai from Okayama Prefecture that appears on rainy nights, rubbing its body against the shins of walking people or slipping between their legs. Because it gets tangled with people's feet while they walk, it sometimes causes them to trip. and when someone tries to catch it, it runs away.

雷獣

[*Raijū* (Thunder Beast)]

雷鳴とともに空から現れ、その爪痕を地上に残します。
A beast that appears from the sky with thunder and leaves its claw marks on the ground.

雷とともに天から降りてくる犬のような姿で、鋭い爪がついた2本の前足と、水かきのついた後足が4本あります。落雷時には雷獣が大暴れし、雷が落ちた木などには雷獣の爪痕が残されていたという話もあります。

A dog-like creature that descends from the heavens with thunder, having two front legs with sharp claws and four webbed hind legs. It is said that when lightning strikes, the *Raijū* goes on a rampage, and stories tell of its claw marks being found on trees or objects that have been struck by the lightning.

COLUMN

安倍晴明

Abe no Seimei

中国から伝わった陰陽道を使って祈祷や占いを行う陰陽師の中で特に有名なのが安倍晴明(あべのせいめい)（921–1005年）です。晴明は、天皇の長引く頭痛が「前世の頭の骨が岩に挟まっているため」と言い当てて治癒をしたり、藤原道長(ふじわらのみちなが)（966–1028年）にかけられた呪いを祓ったりするなど、人間離れした逸話がたくさん残されています。「式神（使い魔）」を自由に操り、天文学や呪術を極めた晴明は、天皇家や朝廷に仕える人々から厚い信頼がありました。厄除けや魔除けのために、京都の晴明神社(せいめいじんじゃ)にはたくさんの人が訪れます。

Among the *ommyōji* (practitioners of *ommyōdō*) who performed prayers and divination using the Chinese-derived art of *ommyōdō*, *Abe no Seimei* (921-1005) is particularly famous. Many supernatural stories remain about *Seimei*, such as correctly diagnosing that the Emperor's persistent headache was "due to a skull from a previous life being trapped between rocks" and curing it, or dispelling curses cast on *Fujiwara no Michinaga* (966-1028). *Seimei*, who could freely control *shikigami* (familiar spirits) and mastered astronomy and sorcery, earned deep trust from the imperial family and court nobles. Many people visit the Seimei Shrine in Kyoto Prefecture for protection against misfortune and evil spirits.

覚

[*Satori*]

大きなサルのような姿で、人の心を読みます。
Takes the form of a large ape and can read human minds.

相手の気持ちを言い当てながら、隙をうかがって人を食おうとします。捕まえようとすると、それを察して素早く逃げてしまいます。心を読むのは得意ですが、予想外のことは苦手で、猟師や木こりのところに現れ、襲うチャンスを狙いますが、たき木が飛んで覚にぶつかると「思わぬことが起きた」と言いながら逃げたという伝承が残っています。

While accurately reading people's feelings, it looks for opportunities to eat humans. When someone tries to catch it, it senses their intention and quickly escapes. Though skilled at reading minds, it's poor at handling unexpected situations. According to legend, it would appear before hunters and woodcutters seeking chances to attack, but if a burning piece of firewood happened to hit it, it would flee while saying, "Something unexpected happened."

狒々

[*Hihi*]

人を食べる巨大なサルの妖怪です。
A giant ape yokai that eats humans.

体長3mほどある怪力のサルで、年を重ねたサルが狒々になります。山で人を見つけると物凄いスピード追いかけて、食べます。人を食べる前に必ず「ヒヒ」と笑うため、この名前になったともいわれています。

The *hihi* is a super-strong ape about 3 meters in length, which forms when a normal ape grows old. When it spots humans in the mountains, it pursues them at incredible speed and devours them. It is said that the name "*Hihi*" comes from the fact that it always laughs before eating its victims, mimicking the sound "*hihi*."

件

[*Kudan*]

牛の体に人間の頭の奇怪な姿で、予言をします。
A bizarre creature with a cow's body and human head that makes prophecies.

生まれてすぐに予言をすると、死んでしまいます。世の中が不安定になると姿を現します。戦争や災害、疫病など、悪い出来事を予言し、その予言は決して外れません。件が描かれた瓦版は厄除けに使われました。

It dies immediately after making its prophecy at birth. It appears when society becomes unstable. It prophesizes negative events such as wars, disasters, and epidemics, and its prophecies never fail to come true. Woodblock prints featuring the *kudan* were used as talismans to ward off misfortune.

下がり

[*Sagari*]

夜道を行く人を、鳴き声で驚かせる馬の首の妖怪です。
A horse-head yokai that startles people walking on night roads with its cry.

樹齢の長いエノキの木からぶらさがる馬の首の妖怪です。鳴き声をあげて、夜道を歩く人を驚かせます。九州では見ると熱病にかかるといわれています。ほかにも似たような妖怪がいます。

A yokai in the form of a horse's head that hangs from ancient hackberry trees. It startles people walking at night with its crying sound. In Kyūshū Region, it is said that seeing one will cause you to catch a fever. There are other similar yokai as well.

COLUMN

予言獣

Yogenjū (Prophetic Beasts)

江戸時代の後期、覚（P96）や件（P99）、アマビエ、などの未来について忠告する予言獣が九州地方に出現し、その記録が図入りで残されています。アマビエは長い髪でくちばしのある人魚のような生き物でした。農作物の出来や疫病などこれから起こる出来事を予言し、「私の姿を写して見ていれば助かる」と伝えます。

In the late Edo-era, prophetic beasts that gave warnings about the future, such as *Satori* (p. 96), *Kudan* (p. 99), and *Amabie*, appeared in the Kyūshū Region, and records of them remain with illustrations. *Amabie* was a mermaid-like creature with long hair and a beak. It prophesized upcoming events such as crop yields and epidemics, and told people, "If you draw and look at my image, you will be saved."

Part 5

鳥・虫・魚などの姿

Birds, Insects, Fish, and Other Creatures' Forms

鳥や虫、魚なども妖怪になります。龍のように信仰されるものもいます。

Even birds, insects, and fish can become yokai. Some, like *ryū*, are worshipped as deities.

104
ヤマタノオロチ
Yamata no Orochi

106
野槌
Nozuchi

107
大蝦蟇
Ōgama

108 八咫烏
Yatagarasu

110 土蜘蛛
Tsuchigumo

112 女郎蜘蛛
Jorōgumo

114 龍
Ryū

116 虯
Mizuchi

117 大百足
Ōmukade

118 岩魚坊主
Iwana-bōzu

119 三尸虫
Sanshi-chū

120 恙虫
Tsutsugamushi

121 網剪
Amikiri

103

ヤマタノオロチ

[*Yamata no Orochi* (Eight-Headed Serpent)]

1つの体に8つの頭と尻尾をもつ、巨大なヘビです。
A giant serpent with eight heads and tails on a single body.

山8つ分くらいの大きなヘビで、体には苔や木が生えています。目はほおずきのように赤く、お腹はいつも血で真っ赤にただれています。毎年、1人ずつ娘を食べていました。お酒をたくさん飲んで、寝たところをスサノオノミコトによって退治されました。出雲の斐伊川周辺にはヤマタノオロチが住んでいた天ヶ淵や、8つの首を埋めたとする8本杉などがあります。

A massive serpent, about the size of eight mountains, with moss and trees growing on its body. Its eyes glowed red like *hōzuki* (Chinese lantern plants), and its belly was always raw and crimson with blood. Each year, it devoured one maiden. It was ultimately slain by *Susano-o no Mikoto* after drinking too much *sake* and falling asleep. Around the Hii River in Izumo, there are places associated with *Yamata no Orochi*, such as Amagafuchi, where it was said to have lived, and *Happon-sugi* (the Eight Cedars), where its eight heads were supposedly buried.

野槌

[*Nozuchi*]

顔がなく、ヘビのような形をした妖怪です。
A yokai with no face and a snake-like form.

頭から尻尾まで同じ太さで、持ち手のないトンカチのような姿をしています。人を見ると坂を転がり降りて襲いにきます。坂を登るのは遅いので、出会ったら高い所に逃げるのがよいとされています。

It has the same thickness from head to tail, and looks like a hammer without a handle. When it sees people, it rolls down slopes to attack them. Since it's slow at climbing slopes, it's said that if you encounter one, it's best to escape to higher ground.

大蝦蟇

[Ōgama (Giant Toad)]

山奥に住む体長 2m 半ほどの大きなガマガエルです。
A huge toad about 2.5 meters long that lives deep in the mountains.

口から虹色の妖気を吐き、虫や鳥、ときには人までも吸い込んでしまいます。また人が岩と間違えてその上に乗ってしまう話が多く残されていて、美女などに化ける妖術を身につけているものもいました。

It breathes out rainbow-colored supernatural energy from its mouth, sucking in insects, birds, and sometimes even humans. There are many stories of people mistaking it for a rock and sitting on it. Some were also known to possess magical powers that allowed them to transform into beautiful women.

八咫烏

[*Yatagarasu*]

足が3本ある大きなカラスで、神様の使いです。

A large crow with three legs that serves as a divine messenger.

熊野(くまの)の神様の使いで、神武天皇(じんむてんのう)が日本を統一しているときに熊野から大和(やまと)まで案内しました。日本では月にはウサギ、太陽には八咫烏が住んでいるとされています。3本の足はそれぞれ「天・地・人」を表しています。

As a messenger of the god of Kumano, it guided Emperor *Jimmu* from Kumano area to Yamato area when he was unifying Japan. In Japanese belief, while a rabbit lives on the moon, the *Yatagarasu* dwells in the sun. Its three legs symbolize "Heaven, Earth, and Humanity."

COLUMN

ツチノコ

Tsuchinoko

日本の UMA ではツチノコが最も有名です。ツチノコは体長 30 〜 80cm の太い胴のヘビのような見た目をしています。人を見れば襲ってくる、人の前に転がってくる、毒があるなどといわれ、日本全国に目撃情報があります。野槌（P106）と似たような生物だと考えられています。

The *Tsuchinoko* is the most famous UMA (Unidentified Mysterious Animal) in Japan. It has a snake-like appearance with a thick body measuring 30-80 cm in length. It's said to attack people when spotted, roll towards humans, and be venomous. Sightings have been reporeted across Japan. It's thought to be similar to the *Nozuchi* (p. 106).

土蜘蛛

[*Tsuchigumo* (Dirt Spider)]

怪しい術を使う巨大なクモです。
A giant spider that uses sinister magic.

怪しい術で人を病気にしたり、人間を食べたりする大きなクモの姿をした妖怪です。源 頼光(P28-29)によって退治された巨大土蜘蛛が有名で、能や歌舞伎の演目にもなっています。北野天満宮の近くには、土蜘蛛が住んでいたという「土蜘蛛塚」が残っています。中世の古い絵巻には、切り裂いた腹からたくさんの人骨があふれ出ている様子が描かれています。

A yokai in the form of a large spider that devours humans or uses dark magic to make them ill. The giant *Tsuchigumo*, which was slain by *Minamoto no Raikō* (pp. 28-29), is particularly famous and appears in *Noh* and *Kabuki* performances. Near Kitano Temmangū Shrine, there is a small mound called "*Tsuchigumo-zuka*" where the creature is said to have lived. In medieval picture scrolls, it is depicted with human bones spilling out of its cut-open belly.

女郎蜘蛛

[*Jorōgumo* (Seductress Spider)]

美しい女性に化けるクモの妖怪です。
A spider yokai that transforms into a beautiful woman.

滝の近くで休んでいる男性の足に糸を巻きつけて、水の中に引き込もうとします。静岡の浄蓮の滝や宮城の賢淵には女郎蜘蛛の伝説が残っていて、男性が足に巻きついた糸を近くの木に結びつけ、代わりに木が水の中に引き込まれ、助かったといいます。ほかにも、美しい女性の姿に化けて男性に結婚を迫ったという話が残っています。

It spins its web around the legs of men resting near waterfalls and tries to drag them into the water. Legends of the *Jorōgumo* remain at Jōren Falls in Shizuoka Prefecture and Kashikobuchi in Miyagi Prefecture. In both places, it is said that a man once survived by tying the thread wrapped around his leg to a nearby tree, which was then pulled into the water instead. Other tales tell of the creature transforming into a beautiful woman and pressuring a man into marriage.

龍

[*Ryū* (Dragon)]

ヘビのような体の、善も悪も備えた存在です。
Beings with snake-like bodies that possesses both good and evil qualities.

ヘビに似て細長く、翼や手足、角などがあるものや、ないものがいて、姿はその龍によってさまざまです。毒龍や大蛇などと呼ばれ、洪水のような災害レベルの被害を与える悪いものがいる一方で、龍神と呼ばれ、人間の願いを叶えてくれるよいものもいます。インドや中国と同じく水の神として古くから信仰の対象となっています。

They have a snake-like thin form but, while some have wings, limbs, and horns, others do not. Their appearance varies depending on the *ryū*. Some are called *dokuryū* (poisonous dragons) or *daija* (giant serpents), bringing disaster-level damage like floods. Others are known as *ryūjin* (dragon gods) who grant human wishes. Like in India and China, they have long been objects of worship as water gods.

虬

[*Mizuchi*]

3mくらいの大きさで龍の仲間です。
A member of the *ryū* family, about 3 meters in size.

土の中で卵から孵り、天に昇るといいます。土砂崩れや洪水の原因でもあります。岡山の高梁(たかはし)には住んでいた虬の毒気で道行く人々が死んでいたので、退治されたという話があります。シカに化けたり魚を引き連れていたりしました。

Mizuchi are said to hatch from eggs in the earth and ascend to the heavens. They can cause landslides and floods. In Takahashi, Okayama Prefecture, there is a story of a *Mizuchi* being exterminated because its poisonous breath was killing passersby. They could also transform into deer and were known to lead schools of fish.

大百足

[*Ōmukade* (Giant Centipede)]

大きなムカデの妖怪で、大蛇とは対立関係です。
A giant centipede yokai that has an antagonistic relationship with giant serpents.

橋に間違えられるくらいの大きさや、山を7巻半したくらいの大きさといわれていて、通る人々に悪さをしています。大蛇とは争っていることが多く、手足の多さで大百足の方が優位に立っています。

It is said to be so massive that people mistake it for a bridge, or large enough to coil around a mountain seven and a half times, and causes mischief to passing people. Frequently engaged in battles with giant serpents, the *Ōmukade* often gains the upper hand due to its many legs.

岩魚坊主

[*Iwana-bōzu* (Char Monk)]

年を取ったイワナが人に化け、説教をします。
An elderly char transforms into a human and gives a lecture.

川に毒を流して魚を獲ろうしている人の前に現れ、やめさせようとします。ご飯をたくさん食べさせると帰ってくれますが、その後の毒流しで獲ったイワナの一匹の胃袋から坊主にあげたご飯が出てきて坊主の正体がイワナだったとわかります。

A monk appears before a man fishing by poisoning a river and tries to convince him to stop. When fed plenty of food, the monk leaves. Later, when the man examines the stomach contents of a char he caught using poison, he sees the food that he gave the monk and realizes that he was actually a char in disguise.

三尸虫

[*Sanshi-chū* (Three Body Worms)]

人の悪事を定期的に神様に告げ口する虫の妖怪です。
Yokai that regularly report a person's misdeeds to the gods.

人の腹の中にいる3匹の虫です。60日ごとに人が眠ると体から抜けて天に昇り、その人が犯した罪を神様に報告します。三尸虫が報告することで命が減ると考えられていたため、60日ごとに集まって眠らないように夜通し飲み食いしました。

These are three worm yokai that live inside a person's belly. Every 60 days, they escape from the person's body while they sleep and ascend to heaven to report the person's sins to the gods. It was believed that these reports from the *Sanshi-chū* would shorten one's life, so people would gather every 60 days to eat and drink all night to avoid sleeping.

恙虫

[*Tsutsugamushi*]

眠っている人の血を吸って死に至らしめる虫の妖怪です。
An insect-like yokai that sucks the blood of sleeping people and can cause death.

ダニのような虫で、眠っている人の血を吸います。恙虫に血を吸われた人は病気になり、酷くなると死んでしまいます。科学が発展したことで原因となったダニが発見され、そのダニに「ツツガムシ」と名付けられました。

A mite-like insect that sucks the blood of sleeping people. Those bitten by the *Tsutsugamushi* become ill and in severe cases may die. With the advancement of science, the mite responsible for the illness was discovered and named "*Tsutsugamushi*"(scrub typhus mite).

網剪

[*Amikiri* (Net Cutter)]

大きなハサミをもつエビのような妖怪です。
A shrimp-like yokai that has large pincers.

鳥山石燕(とりやませきえん)(P145)による妖怪画集『画図百鬼夜行(がずひゃっきやこう)』に描かれた妖怪で、エビに似た体にカニのような大きなハサミ、鳥のようなクチバシをもっています。漁に使う網や蚊帳を切り刻んで人々を困らせます。

A creature depicted in *Toriyama Sekien*'s yokai art collection *Gazu Hyakki Yakō*, it has a shrimp-like body with large crab-like pincers and a bird-like beak. It trobules people by cutting up fishing nets and mosquito nets.

COLUMN

いろいろな龍

Various *Ryū*

日本にはドラゴンのようなトカゲの姿をした龍はほとんどいません。龍はヘビのような姿をしていて、ヤマタノオロチ（P104-105）や虬（P116）も龍の一種とされています。ほかにも、9つの頭がある九頭竜や、片目が見えない一つ目龍、雷を放ったり人の姿になったりできるカンナカムイ、大きなほら貝に龍が入った姿の出世螺など、たくさんの龍が日本にいます。龍の多くは水を操ったり雨を降らせたり、人の言葉がわかったりするといわれています。

In Japan, there are very few *ryū* that look like lizards, as they are typically depicted in the West. *Ryū* have snake-like forms, and creatures like the *Yamata no Orochi* (pp. 104-105) and *Mizuchi* (p. 116) are considered types of *ryū*. There are many other types of *ryū* in Japan, including the nine-headed *Kuzuryū*; the one-eyed *Hitotsume Ryū*; the *Kanna-kamui* that can release lightning and change into human form; and the *Shusse-bora* that takes the form of a *ryū* inside a large conch shell. Most *ryū* are said to be able to control water, make rain fall, and understand human speech.

Part 6

物の姿
Object Forms

お皿や傘、刀、鏡などの、物体も妖怪になります。
Objects such as plates, umbrellas, swords, and mirrors can also become yokai.

126 付喪神
Tsukumogami

130 傘お化け
Kasa-obake

132 提灯お化け
Chōchin-obake

133 一反木綿
Ittan-momen

134 目目蓮
Mokumokuren

135 雲外鏡
Ungaikyō

136 妖刀村正
Yotō Muramasa

140 朧車
Oboroguruma

141 鳴釜
Narikama

142 迷い家
Mayoiga

144 化け地蔵
Bake-jizō

125

付喪神

[*Tsukumogami* (Possessed Tools)]

長い間使われた道具が妖怪となったものです。
Tools and objects that have turned into yokai after being used for many years.

Part 6 Object Forms

捨てられた道具や器物が妖怪となって、ものを大切にしない人に対して仕返しをします。日本では昔から長い間使われた道具や器物には精霊が宿り、怪しい力が使えるようになると考えられていて、しゃもじや布団、枕、すりこぎなどの生活用品に顔や手足が生えて化けたという話が残っています。「九十九神」と書くこともあります。

Discarded tools and utensils transform into yokai and take revenge on people who don't take care of their belongings. In Japan, it has long been believed that tools and utensils used for many years would become inhabited by spirits and gain mysterious powers. There are stories of everyday items like rice paddles, futons, pillows, and grinding pestles growing faces and limbs and transforming into yokai. It is also written as "ninty-nine gods" in *kanji* and read *Tsukumogami*.

COLUMN

付喪神絵巻

Picture Scroll of the *Tsukumogami*

付喪神（P126-127）の話が書かれた絵巻物に『付喪神絵巻』というものがあります。付喪神絵巻には、捨てられた古い道具たちが妖怪になって、人間に仕返しをしましたが退治され、改心して成仏するまでの物語が絵と一緒に書かれています。人間への仕返しに成功してお祭り騒ぎをしたり、付喪神同士でケンカしたり人間のようなふるまいをしています。現在残っているものの中で最も古いといわれている室町時代に作られたものが岐阜の崇福寺に保管されています。江戸時代以降に多く模写されてきました。

There is an illustrated scroll called *Tsukumogami Emaki* that tells the story of *Tsukumogami* (pp. 126-127). It depicts a tale of discarded old tools that transform into yokai and attempt revenge on humans. But after being defeated, they repent and ultimately achieve Buddhist enlightenment. The scroll portrays them acting like humans, such as fighting amongst themselves or celebrating having successfully taken revenge on humans. The oldest known version of this scroll dates from the Muromachi-era and is preserved at Sōfukuji Temple in Gifu Prefecture. It has been widely copied since the Edo-era.

出典：国立国会図書館「イメージバンク」

傘お化け

[*Kasa-obake* (Umbrella Spirit)]

１つの目（または２つの目）がついた古い唐傘の妖怪です。

A yokai that is an old paper umbrella with one eye (or sometimes two eyes).

2本の手と1本の足が生えていて、ピョンピョンと跳ね回って人を驚かします。絵本やかるたや歌舞伎、お化け屋敷などにも登場する有名な妖怪ですが、実際の目撃情報はほとんどなく、絵画上にのみ存在する妖怪ともいわれます。また、長く使われた生活用品が人に捨てられて化ける付喪神（P 126-127）の一種とも考えられています。

It has two arms and one leg that grow from it, and it hops around startling people. While it's a famous yokai that appears in picture books, *karuta* cards, *kabuki* plays, and haunted houses, there are almost no actual reported sightings, and it's said to exist only in artwork. It's also considered to be a type of *Tsukumogami* (pp. 126-127), objects that transform into yokai after being used for many years and then discarded by people.

提灯お化け

[*Chōchin-obake* (Lantern Ghost)]

破けた提灯が人の顔になり、人々を驚かします。
A torn paper lantern that becomes a human face and startles people.

古びて破けた提灯が大きく上下に割れ、そこが口になって舌が出て目鼻がついた妖怪です。「お化け」として象徴的に描かれるキャラクターですが、各地に伝承などは残っておらず、キツネやタヌキが化けたものや怪火の1つと考えられています。

A yokai that is an old, torn paper lantern that splits widely at the top and bottom, with the split becoming a mouth with a tongue, and growing eyes and a nose. While it's symbolically depicted as a classic *obake* (ghost) character, there are no local folklores about it, and it's thought to be either a transformed fox or *tanuki*, or a type of mysterious fire.

一反木綿

[*Ittan-momen*]

人に巻きついて襲う細長い白い布の妖怪です。
A yokai in the form of a long white strip of cloth that attacks people by wrapping around them.

鹿児島に伝わる妖怪で、１反（長さ10m60cm、幅30cm）の白い布が夕暮れ時にヒラヒラと空を飛び、人の体や首に巻きついたり、そのまま飛び去ったりします。夕方遅くまで遊んでいる子どもに「一反木綿が出るよ」と帰宅を促しました。

A yokai from Kagoshima Prefecture that appears as *ittan* (one tan) of white cloth strip. *ittan* (one *tan*) in length 10.6 meters long and 30cm wide that flutters through the air at dusk, wrapping itself around people's bodies and necks, or sometimes flying away with them. Parents would warn children who played outside until late, saying "The *Ittan-momen* will come out!" to get them to return home.

目目蓮

[*Mokumokuren*]

障子の中にびっしりと現れる目の妖怪です。

A yokai that appears as many tightly packed eyes within sliding paper doors.

家の障子にたくさんの目がびっしりと浮かび上がる妖怪で、人を驚かす以外は特に悪さをしません。目目蓮に遭遇した江戸の商人が障子に現れた目を集めて持ち帰り、眼科医に売ったという逸話が残っています。

This is a yokai that manifests as numerous densely packed eyes floating on household *shoji* doors. It doesn't cause any particular mischief besides startling people. There's an anecdote about an Edo period merchant who encountered a *Mokumokuren*, collected the eyes that appeared on the *shoji*, took them home, and sold them to an eye doctor.

雲外鏡

[*Ungaikyō*]

魔物の正体を見破る鏡の妖怪です。

A yokai mirror that reveals the true identity of demons.

鳥山石燕(とりやませきえん)(P145)によって描かれた妖怪で、中国の伝説の鏡「照魔鏡」と同じような能力があるといわれています。照魔鏡は王様を陥れるために王妃に化けた九尾の狐(P82)の正体を見破ったとされています。

A yokai, drawn by *Toriyama Sekien*, said to have abilities similar to the legendary Chinese mirror, the *Shōmakyō* (Demon-Revealing Mirror). The *Shōmakyō* is said to have revealed the true identity of the *Kyūbi no Kitsune* (p. 82) that had transformed into an empress in an attempt to bring down the emperor.

妖刀村正

[*Yotō Muramasa* (*Muramasa* the Cursed Sword)]

魔力をもつ妖刀で、人を殺すまで止まりません。
A cursed sword with supernatural powers that won't rest until it takes a life.

刀工の村正(むらまさ)が作った刀は徳川家康(とくがわいえやす)の祖父や父など切ったといわれ、徳川家と因縁があると恐れられました。いつしか不吉な魔力をもつ「妖刀」と呼ばれるようになり、「持つ者に災をもたらす」「人を殺すまで止まらない」などといわれるようになりました。刀工の村正の切れ味と美しさへの強いこだわりが生み出したとされます。

The swords forged by the swordsmith *Muramasa* were said to have cut down *Tokugawa Ieyasu*'s grandfather and father, leading to them being feared as having a sinister connection to the *Tokugawa* family. Over time, they came to be known as "Cursed Sword" possessing ominous supernatural powers, with stories claiming they "bring disaster to their wielders" and "won't stop until they kill someone." These legends are said to have emerged from swordsmith *Muramasa*'s intense obsession with creating blades of supreme sharpness and beauty.

COLUMN

日本のエクスキャリバー

Japan's Excalibur

エクスキャリバーといえばアーサー王の魔法の剣が有名ですが、日本にも天皇の証として代々引き継がれる三種の神器の中に「草薙剣(くさなぎのつるぎ)」という伝説の剣があります。スサノオノミコトが倒したヤマタノオロチの尻尾から出てきたもので、アマテラスオオミカミに献上されました。その後、日本を統一する旅に出たヤマトタケルノミコトに託されました。旅の途中、炎に巻かれたヤマトタケルノミコトを救ったとされています。現在は愛知にある熱田神宮(あつたじんぐう)の御神体として祀られています。

While Excalibur is a famous magical sword of King Arthur, Japan has its own legendary sword called *Kusanagi no Tsurugi*, one of three sacred treasures passed down through generations as proof of imperial succession. It emerged from the tail of the *Yamata no Orochi* after it was slain by *Susano-o no Mikoto*, who then presented it to *Amaterasu Ōmikami*. Later, it was entrusted to

Yamato Takeru no Mikoto during his journey to unify Japan. During *Yamato Takeru no Mikoto*'s travels, it is said that the sword saved his life when he was engulfed in flames. Today, it is enshrined as a sacred object of worship at Atsuta Shrine in Aichi Prefecture.

朧車

[*Oboroguruma* (Hazy Ox Cart)]

馬の頭をした鬼が貼りついた牛車の妖怪です。

A yokai in the form of an ox cart with a demonic horse head attached to it.

夜中に車輪をきしませて走る牛車です。たくさんの牛車がある道を無理矢理通ったせいでボロボロになった恨みから妖怪になりました。牛車は、車輪のついた屋形を牛に引かせる平安時代の貴族の乗り物です。

It's an ox cart that runs at night making creaking wheel sounds. It became a yokai due to its resentment after being damaged from being forcefully driven through crowded areas with many other ox carts. The ox cart was a Heian period nobleman's mode of transport consisting of a wheeled carriage pulled by an ox.

鳴釜

[*Narikama* (Sounding Cauldron)]

釜をかぶった毛だらけの妖怪です。

A hairy yokai wearing a cooking pot on its head.

「鳴り釜」という占いの際に釜を鳴らす妖怪です。鳴り釜は釜で米を蒸すときに出る音で願い事が叶うかどうかを占う方法で、古くから行われてきました。岡山にある吉備津神社では「鳴釜神事」と呼ばれ、今も続いています。

This is a yokai that makes cooking pots ring during a form of divination called *Narikama*. *Narikama* divination is an ancient practice that involves interpreting the sounds made by a pot while steaming rice to determine whether wishes will come true. At Kibitsu Shrine in Okayama Prefecture, this practice has continued until today as a ritual called *Narikama Shinji*.

迷い家

[*Mayoiga*]

行こうと思ったら行けない幻の家です。
A phantom house that cannot be reached intentionally.

関東〜東北地方に伝わる山の中にある家です。行こうと思っても行くことができず、偶然迷い込むことでしかこの家に行くことはできません。家の中にある火鉢には湯気が立った鉄瓶がかけてあり、馬小屋には馬もいますが、人の姿はありません。家の中にあるものをなんでもいいので持ち帰ると幸せになれるといわれています。

This is a mysterious house in the mountains that appears in folklore from the Kantō to Tōhoku Regions. One cannot reach it deliberately - it can only be found by accidentally wandering into it. Inside, there is a brazier with a steaming iron kettle, and there's even a horse in the stable, but no human presence can be found. It's said that taking anything from inside the house will bring good fortune.

化け地蔵

[*Bake-jizō*]

行きと帰りで数が違う地蔵です。
Jizō statues whose numbers differ between your outward and return journey.

栃木の憾満ヶ淵にはたくさんの地蔵が並んでいる道があります。行くときと帰るときで数が違うといわれ「化け地蔵」と呼ばれています。もともとは100体の地蔵がありましたが、1902年の大洪水で流されて70体ほどが残っています。

In Kanmangafuchi in Tochigi Prefecture, there is a path lined with many *Jizō* statues. They are called *Bake-jizō* because their numbers are said to differ between when you go and when you return. Originally, there were 100 statues, but after a great flood in 1902, only about 70 remain.

COLUMN

鳥山石燕の妖怪画
Toriyama Sekien's Yokai Art

現在イメージされている妖怪の姿の多くは江戸時代中期に活躍した画家の鳥山石燕(とりやませきえん)（1712〜1788年）が描いたものが大きく影響しています。石燕は図鑑のような形式で描いた妖怪画を多く残していて、古くから伝わってきた妖怪のほかにも石燕が新しく作り出した妖怪もいます。

Many of the yokai images we recognize today were greatly influenced by the artworks of *Toriyama Sekien* (1712-1788), who was active during the mid-Edo-era. *Sekien* left behind numerous yokai illustrations in an encyclopedia-like format. It includs not only traditional yokai that have been passed down through the ages but also new yokai that he created himself.

出展：国立国会図書館「イメージバンク」

Part 7

さまざまな姿
Various Forms

いろいろな生き物やものの特徴を合わせもったキメラのような妖怪です。
They are chimera-like yokai that combine the characteristics of various creatures and objects.

河童

[*Kappa*]

手に水かき、頭に皿、口にくちばしがあります。
Has webbed hands, a dish on its head, and a beak for a mouth.

頭に皿を乗せた子どものような容姿が特徴的ですが、地域によってはカワウソやカメのような姿だと信じられてきました。人と相撲を取ることとキュウリが大好きです。子どもを水に引き込むので、今でも川での遊泳禁止の看板に河童が描かれることがあります。その一方で河童は多くの町のマスコットキャラクターとして親しまれています。

Though typically depicted with a child-like appearance and a dish on its head, in some regions it has been believed to look like an otter or turtle. It's believed to love cucumbers and *sumō* wrestling with humans. Because it pulls children into the water, even today some swimming prohibition signs near rivers feature images of *kappa*. On the other hand, *kappa* also serve as familiar mascot characters for many towns.

木霊

[*Kodama*]

長生きした樹木には精霊が宿るといわれます。
It is said that ancient trees harbor these spirits.

100年以上の樹齢がある木に宿る精霊・木の精です。古くから長く生きた木は大切に扱われ、無闇に切り倒そうとすると祟られるといわれることも多いです。伐採前にお祈りやお祭りを行う風習は日本各地で見られます。

Kodama are spirits that may inhabit trees over 100 years old. Since ancient times, long-lived trees have been treated with great care, and it's often said that cutting them down carelessly will result in being cursed. The custom of performing prayers and ceremonies before logging can be found throughout Japan.

がしゃ髑髏

[*Gashadokuro*]

野垂れ死んだ人の骨が集まって巨大な骸骨に。
A giant skeleton formed from the gathered bones of people who died unattended in the open.

墓に埋葬されなかった人や野垂れ死んだ人たちの骨が集まり、巨大な骸骨になったといわれる妖怪です。深夜2時頃、がしゃがしゃと音を立てながらさまよい、人を食うとされています。歌川国芳の「相馬の古内裏」の浮世絵が有名です。

This is a yokai said to be formed when the bones of unburied people and those who died in the open gather together to create a giant skeleton. Around 2 a.m., it wanders around making rattling noises and is said to devour people. It is famously depicted in *Utagawa Kuniyoshi*`s *ukiyo-e Sōma no Furudairi* (The Ancient Palace of Soma).

山彦

[*Yamabiko* (Mountain Echo)]

人々の呼びかけに少し遅れて返す、見えない妖怪。
An invisible yokai that returns people's calls with a slight delay.

山に向かって声かけたり音を出したりすると、少し遅れてその音が返ってくる「こだま現象」は、山彦や木霊が応える声だと考えられてきました。高知の宿毛市では昼でも夜でも山深い地域で突然聞こえる声のことを「ヤマヒコ」と呼び、恐れられています。中国から伝わる木の精・彭侯は犬のような姿をしており、山彦と同一視されることもあります。

The "echo phenomenon," where sounds and voices called toward mountains return slightly delayed, has traditionally been thought to be the response of *yamabiko*. In Sukumo City, Kochi Prefecture, sudden voices heard in deep mountain areas both day and night are called "*Yamahiko*" and are feared. The Chinese tree spirit *hōkō*, which has a dog-like appearance, is sometimes thought of as being the same as the *Yamabiko*.

火車

[*Kasha* (Fire Chariot)]

火車は死者を奪い、地獄の車に乗せて去ります。
The *Kasha* steals the dead and takes them to hell in its chariot.

葬式や死者を送る葬列から死体を奪っていく妖怪です。生前に悪いことをした人を乗せて地獄に運ぶ車や、地獄の番人が責め苦に使う車のことを「火車」といい、妖怪の火車もこの車に乗せて奪った死人を運ぶと考えられています。猫は魔性の動物で死者に近づくと生き返らせるなどといわれてきたことから、火車の正体は猫という説も多く伝わっています。

This is a yokai that steals corpses during funerals and from funeral processions. The term *kasha* refers both to a chariot that carries evil people to hell after death and to one that is used by hell's guardians for torture. It's believed that this yokai *Kasha* uses such a chariot to transport the dead bodies it steals. Additionally, since cats have traditionally been considered mystical animals, capable of bewitching and reviving the dead, many theories suggest that the true identity of the *Kasha* is actually a cat.

COLUMN

地獄にちなむ土地

Places Associated with Hell

温泉や火山によって地面から煙が噴き出していて、地獄のような風景を見ることができる場所が日本各地にあります。
北海道の登別地獄谷では、噴き出す火山ガスによって近くの岩が黄色っぽくなったり、硫黄の匂いがしていたり、周りの植物が枯れていたりと、まさに地獄のような景色です。
大分の別府では、赤い温泉が湧き出す血の池地獄や、泥が沸とうしている鬼石坊主地獄など、7つの地獄をまわる、地獄めぐりが人気です。

There are places throughout Japan where smoke rises from the ground due to hot springs and volcanoes, creating landscapes reminiscent of hell. At Noboribetsu Jigokudani (Hell Valley) in Hokkaido Prefecture, volcanic gases emit sulfuric odors, make nearby rocks appear yellowish, and kill surrounding vegetation, creating a truly hell-like landscape.

In Beppu, Oita Prefecture, the popular *Jigoku Meguri* (hell tour) takes visitors to seven different hells, including the Chinoike Jigoku (Blood Pond Hell), where red hot springs bubble up, and the Oniishi Bōzu Jigoku (Shaven Monk's Head Hell) where mud boils.

海坊主

[*Umibōzu* (Sea Monk)]

真っ黒の巨大な入道姿で船に襲いかかります。

A giant, pitch-black monk-like creature that attacks ships.

真っ黒く大きな坊主頭の海の妖怪で、その体は大きいものになると30mもあるといいます。突然海の中から現れ、船を壊して沈没させたり、人を海に引きずり込んだり、ときには船幽霊（P48-49）のように「柄杓を貸せ」と言うものもいます。

This is a sea yokai with a large, black shaved head, and its body is said to sometimes reach up to 30 meters in size. It suddenly appears from the sea, destroying and sinking ships, dragging people into the water, and sometimes, like the *Funayūrei* (pp. 48-49), it demands, "Lend me your ladle."

釣瓶下ろし

[*Tsurube-oroshi* (Dropping Well Bucket)]

木の上から落ちてきて、下を歩く人を食べます。

A yokai that falls from trees to attack and eat people walking below.

木から釣瓶（井戸の桶）や生首が落ちてきて、歩く人を襲ったり、食べたりするという妖怪です。京都の釣瓶下ろしは「夜なべ済んだか、釣瓶おろそか、ギイギイ」と言いながら、降りてきます。地域によっては、松明や鍋が落ちてきます。

A yokai that drops from trees, resembling either a well bucket (*tsurube*) or a severed head, attacking or eating those passing underneath. In Kyoto Prefecture, the *Tsurube-oroshi* is said to descend while chanting, "Have you finished your night work? Shall I drop *Tsurube*? Creak, creak." In some regions, torches or pots are said to fall instead.

鵺

[*Nue*]

いろいろな動物の体の部位をもっています。

A yokai with body parts from various animals.

サルの頭、タヌキの体、手足がトラ、尾はヘビの姿をした妖怪です。『平家物語(へいけものがたり)』の中で弓の名手の源 頼政(みなもとのよりまさ)に退治される話が有名です。その遺骸を船に乗せて流し、漂着したとされる鵺塚(ぬえづか)が兵庫の芦屋市(あしやし)にあります。

The *nue* is a yokai with a monkey's head, *tanuki*'s body, tiger's limb, and snake's tail. It is famous for being slain by the master archer, *Minamoto no Yorimasa* in The Tale of the Heike. Its remains were placed on a boat and set adrift, eventually washing ashore in Ashiya City, Hyogo Prefecture, where the Nuezuka (*Nue* Mound) now stands.

牛鬼

[*Ushi-oni*]

頭は牛で体は鬼（その反対も）の妖怪です。
A yokai that has an ox's head and *oni's* body (or vice versa).

海岸や湖沼など水辺を歩く人を襲い、食い殺すといわれます。乱暴な性格で毒の気を吐くことから、見るだけ・近くに現れるだけで死ぬこともありました。西日本に多く見られ、愛媛の宇和島市では毎年牛鬼まつりが行われます。

It is said to attack and devour people while they are walking near water, such as coastlines and lakes. Due to its violent nature and poisonous breath, people can die just from seeing it or having it appear nearby. It is commonly found in Western Japan, and in Uwajima City, Ehime Prefecture, annual *Ushi-oni Matsuri* (*Ushi-oni* Festival) is held.

怪火

[*Kaika*]

日本には多種多様な火の玉が飛び交います。
In Japan, many different types of fireballs fly through the air.

怪火は夜などに突然現れ、人を驚かす火の玉です。その種類は多様で、例えば鬼火は人や家畜の死体から生まれた青い火で、人魂は人の魂が浮遊したもの。狐火はキツネたちの集まりの様子で、天狗火は天狗が飛ばす火の玉のこと。多くの場合は人間の霊魂や怨念、妖怪の仕業と考えられており、無害なものから見ただけで死んでしまうものまでさまざまです。

Kaika are mysterious fireballs that suddenly appear, often at night, startling people. They come in many varieties: *Onibi* are blue flames born from human or animal corpses, *Hitodama* are floating human souls, *Kitsunebi* appear when foxes gather, and *Tengubi* are fireballs cast by *tengu*. Most are thought to be manifestations of human spirits, grudges, or yokai mischief. They range from harmless phenomena to those so dangerous that merely seeing them can be fatal.

人魚

[*Ningyo* (Mermaid)]

人魚の肉を食べると不老長寿になるといわれます。

It is said that eating *ningyo* flesh grants immortality and eternal youth.

福井の小浜市には人魚の肉を食べて何百年も旅して回った八百比丘尼が永眠する洞窟があるほか、各地にその足跡が残っています。人魚が現れるのは豊作などの吉兆でしたが、次第に津波や暴風雨の前ぶれと恐れられるようになりました。

A cave in Obama City, Fukui Prefecture is said to be the resting place of a nun named *Yaobikuni* who supposedly lived for hundreds of years after eating *ningyo* flesh. Traces of her travails can also be found throughout various regions. While *ningyo* appearances were once considered good omens, such as a sign of a bountiful harvest, they gradually came to be feared as harbingers of tsunamis and violent storms.

ケセランパサラン

[*Keseran Pasaran*]

白い毛玉は人に幸せを運んできます。
White fluffy balls that bring people happiness.

タンポポの綿毛のような白いフワフワとした毛玉で、持ち主に幸せをもたらすといわれている謎の存在です。空中を飛んでいるところを捕獲することもでき、空気穴の開いた桐の箱の中に入れておしろいを与えると、大きく育つこともあります。

A mysterious entity that looks like a white, fluffy ball similar to dandelion fluff, said to bring happiness to its owner. They can be caught while floating through the air and are sometimes kept in boxes made of paulownia wood with air holes. Feeding them face powder is believed to help them grow larger.

Part 8

現代の妖怪
Modern Yokai

うわさ話やインターネットで新たに妖怪や都市伝説が生まれることもあります。
New yokai and urban legends can also emerge from rumors and the internet.

| 168 くねくね *Kune-Kune* | 170 テケテケ *Teke-Teke* | 172 八尺様 *Hasshaku-sama* |

| 174 トイレの花子さん *Toire no Hanako-san* | 178 口裂け女 *Kuchisake-onna* | 179 人面犬 *Jinmen-ken* |

180
メリーさんの電話
Mary's Phone Call

181
3本足のリカちゃん人形
Three-Legged *Licca-chan* Doll

184
きさらぎ駅
Kisaragi Station

186
ヒサルキ
Hisaruki

167

くねくね

[*Kune-Kune* (Wriggler)]

くねくねと体をくねらせる白い物体です。
A white entity that wriggles and twists its body.

2000年頃から日本各地の田んぼや川などの水辺で目撃情報があがり始めた妖怪で、人ではないような動きで体をくねくねさせる白い物体です。遠くから見る程度なら害はありませんが、間近で見てしまうと精神を病んでしまうといわれます。くねくねを見て狂ってしまった人は、その後くねくねに変化するといわれ、気配を感じたら素早く目を逸らすことが大切です。

A yokai that began to be reported around water areas like rice paddies and rivers across Japan around 2000. It appears as a white entity that twists its body in a distinctly non-human manner. Although observing it from a distance may be harmless, it is said that looking at it up close can lead to mental breakdown. People who go insane from seeing the *Kune-Kune* are said to transform into one themselves. If you sense its presence, it's important to quickly look away.

テケテケ

[*Teke-Teke*]

下半身を失った女子中学生が足を探し回ります。
A junior high school girl who searches for her lost legs.

事故で体を真っ二つに切断された女子中学生の上半身が、下半身を探して夜な夜な這い回る亡霊です。両手2本で移動するにも関わらず、その動きは異常なほど素早く、追いつかれるとカマやハサミで襲われて足を奪われるといわれます。這い回るときに「テケテケ」と音を立てることが名前の由来とされており、この話を聞いた人のところにも現れると恐れられています。

This is a ghost of a middle school girl whose body was cut in half in an accident. Her upper body crawls around at night searching for her lower half. Despite moving with only her two hands, her movements are unnaturally fast. And it's said that if she catches you, she'll attack with a sickle or scissors to steal your legs. The name comes from the *"teke-teke"* sound she makes while crawling. And it's feared that she will appear to anyone who hears this story.

八尺様

[*Hasshaku-sama*]

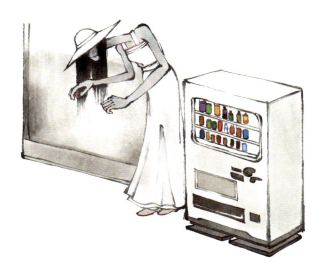

八尺様を見た者は必ず呪い殺されてしまいます。
Those who see *Hasshaku-sama* are inevitably cursed to death.

白いワンピースに白い帽子をかぶった、身長が8尺（2m40cm）もある女性の妖怪。「ぽぽぽ」という機械のような声を発しながら、特に子どもを狙って襲うといわれます。狙った獲物をおびき出すため、知っている人の声色を真似ることも得意です。八尺様に狙われたらどこかに連れ去られるか、数日のうちに呪い殺されるため、八尺様を見た者はこの世に存在しません。

A female yokai who stands eight *shaku* tall (2.4 meters), wearing a white dress and white hat. She emits a mechanical-like sound, "po-po-po" and is said to especially target children. She is skilled at mimicking the voices of people her victims know in order to lure them in. Those targeted by her are either abducted or cursed to die within a few days, meaning that no one who has seen *Hasshaku-sama* remains in this world.

トイレの花子さん

[*Toire no Hanako-san* (*Hanako-san* in the Toilet)]

学校の怪談の中で一番有名な幽霊です。
The most famous ghost among several school ghost stories.

Part 8

Modern Yokai

学校のトイレの3番目の個室で名前を呼ぶと返事をする、おかっぱ頭に赤いスカートの女の子といわれています。3階のトイレ、戸を3回叩く、3回まわるなど、呼び出し方は学校によってさまざまです。その結果、呪われたり、1年で死んだりすることもあります。

Said to be a bob-haired girl in a red skirt who responds when her name, "*Hanako-san*" is called in the third stall of the school restroom. But the method of summoning her varies by school, such as using the third-floor restroom, knocking on the door three times, or spinning around three times. Those who summon her can become cursed or die within a year.

COLUMN

学校の七不思議
The Seven Mysteries of the School

学校にまつわる7つの怖い話を集めた「七不思議」は小学生の定番の怪談です。トイレの花子さん（P174-175）が一番有名で、人体模型が動く、音楽室のベートーベンの肖像画の顔が変わる、楽器がひとりでに鳴る、鏡に何かが映る、体育館でボールが弾む音がする、階段の段数が変わる、入れない部屋があるなどがあります。その学校オリジナルの話が入ることもあります。7つ目を知るとよくないことが起こるとされています。

The "Seven Mysteries" is a collection of scary legends that is a staple among elementary school ghost tales. The specific stories vary by school, but the most famous is *Toire no Hanako-san* (pp. 174-175). Other common tales include a human anatomy model that moves on its own; Beethoven's portrait in the music room changing its expression; instruments playing by themselves;

strange reflections appearing in mirrors; the sound of a ball bouncing in the gymnasium; staircases with changing numbers of steps; and rooms that cannot be entered. Schools also often include original stories unique to their location. It is said that learning about the seventh mystery brings bad luck.

口裂け女

[*Kuchisake-onna* (Slit-Mouthed Woman)]

口が裂けた女性が、自分がきれいか尋ねてきます。

A woman with a slit mouth hidden by a mask who asks if she is beautiful.

赤いコートに大きなマスクをした女性で、道行く人に「私、きれい?」と聞いてきます。「きれい」と答えないと襲ってきますが、「ポマード」と叫ぶと逃げていくともいわれます。出没情報が相次いだ時代は、生徒の集団下校が行われました。

A woman wearing a red coat and a large mask who approaches passersby and asks, "Am I beautiful?" If you don't answer "beautiful," she will attack you. But it is said that shouting "pomade" will make her flee. During a time when sightings of her were reported frequently, walk-home groups for students were organized.

人面犬

[*Jinmen-ken* (The Human-Faced Dog)]

人の言葉を話す、人間の顔をした犬の妖怪です。
A dog yokai with a human face that speaks human language.

顔は人間、体は犬で人の言葉を話す都市伝説上の妖怪です。夜の高速道路で車を追い抜く、繁華街のゴミ箱をあさりながら憎まれ口をきく、という2つの目撃情報が主流。大学の研究室で実験の際に偶発的に生まれたといううわさもあります。

An urban legend yokai with a dog's body and a human face that speaks human language. There are two main types of reported sightings: one where it overtakes cars on highways at night, and another where it rummages through garbage bins in entertainment districts while making sarcastic remarks. There are also rumors that it was accidentally created during an experiment in a university laboratory.

メリーさんの電話

[Mary's Phone Call]

人形のメリーさんが電話のたびに少しずつ近づいてきます。
A doll named Mary gets closer with each phone call.

ある少女が引っ越しの際に捨てた西洋人形の怪異。新しい家の電話を少女が取ると、「私メリー、今ゴミ捨て場にいるの」「駅にいるの」「あなたの家の前にいるの」と徐々に近づき、最後は「今あなたの後ろにいるの」と少女を驚かせます。
A haunting involving a Western-style doll discarded by a girl when she moved house. After relocating, the girl answers the phone at her new home and hears, "This is Mary. I'm at the garbage dump now," followed by subsequent calls saying, "I'm at the station" and, "I'm in front of your house." Then she finally shocks the girl by saying, "I'm right behind you."

3本足のリカちゃん人形

[Three-Legged *Licca-chan* Doll]

呪われたリカちゃんの声がどこまでもついてきます。
The cursed Licca-chan doll's voice follows you relentlessly.

リカちゃん人形は日本の女の子に人気の着せ替え人形です。ある女の子がトイレでリカちゃん人形を拾うと、足が3本あり驚いて落としてしまいます。すると「私リカちゃん、呪われているの」としゃべり続け、女の子は発狂してしまいました。
Licca-chan dress-up dolls are popular among Japanese girls. One day, a girl found a *Licca-chan* doll in a restroom, but she was shocked to find that it had three legs, so she dropped it. The doll then began speaking, saying, "I'm Licca, and I'm cursed," over and over until the girl went insane.

COLUMN

都市伝説

Urban Legends

現代の都市社会で実際に現れたと信じられる妖怪や怪異現象のうわさ話を「都市伝説」と呼びます。1970年代末から社会問題にもなった口裂け女（P178）をはじめ、人面犬（P179）、メリーさんの電話（P180）など、いろいろな話が広まりました。さらに、インターネットが普及した後は口から口へだけでなく「ネットロア」といってネット上で生まれて広がっていく妖怪や異界も現れました。八尺様（P172-173）、きさらぎ駅（P184-185）、ヒサルキ（P186）などがその代表です。

"Urban legends" refers to rumors about yokai and supernatural phenomena believed to have actually appeared in modern society. Various stories spread, starting with *Kuchisake-onna* (p. 178), which became a social issue in the late 1970s, along with *Jinmen-ken* (p. 179) and Mary's Phone Call (p. 180). With the rise of the internet, these legends not only spread by word of mouth but also evolved into "Netlore," supernatural stories born and propagated online. *Hasshaku-sama* (pp. 172-173), *Kisaragi* Station (pp. 184-185), and *Hisaruki* (p. 186) are iconic examples of this.

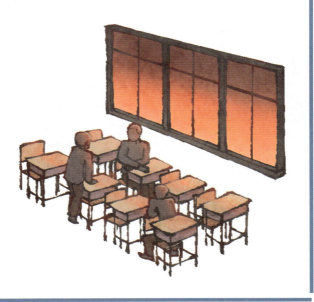

きさらぎ駅

[*Kisaragi* Station]

電車でうたたねをすると実在しない駅に着きます。
If you doze off on a train, you may arrive at this station that doesn't exist.

静岡県の遠州鉄道沿線にあるとされる実在しない駅です。インターネットの掲示板で「はすみ」という女性が「いつもの電車に乗ったはずなのに様子が違う」と投稿し、あるはずのない「きさらぎ駅」で降ります。掲示板上で他の参加者とリアルタイムでやり取りをしながら線路沿いを歩いて戻る間、はすみは不気味な人たちと出会い、結果的に消息を絶ったとされています。

Kisaragi Station is said to be a nonexistent station located along the Enshu Railway Line in Shizuoka Prefecture. The legend originated from an internet forum post by a woman named "*Hasumi*" who claimed, "I boarded my usual train, but something feels off." She reportedly got off at the mysterious "*Kisaragi* Station," a place that should not exist. While interacting with other forum participants in real time, she described her journey walking along the train tracks to find her way back. During this time, she encountered unsettling individuals and ultimately disappeared, leaving her fate unknown.

ヒサルキ

[*Hisaruki*]

子どもが集まる場所で虫や小動物を串刺しにします。
It impales insects and small animals in places where children gather.

幼稚園や保育園など子どもが集まる場所で、柵の先端に虫や爬虫類、小動物をなど串刺しにして自分の痕跡を残す不気味な妖怪です。その姿は子どもにしか見えませんが、子どもに聞いてもどんな姿かを説明できる子はいません。

A disturbing yokai that leaves traces of itself by impaling insects, reptiles, and small animals on fence tops at places where children gather, such as kindergartens and nursery schools. Only children can see it, but when asked, none of them can explain what it looks like.

COLUMN

妖怪のミイラ

Yokai Mummies

江戸時代に見世物小屋に展示するために河童（P148-149）や人魚（P164）など、いろいろな妖怪のミイラが作られました。サルや猫、魚などの生き物を組み合わせて作られたミイラは本物のような出来で、外国に渡ったものもあります。日本では寺や神社、博物館などで保管されています。

During the Edo-era, mummies of various yokai, such as *kappa* (pp. 148-149) and *ningyo*, (p. 164) were created and displayed in carnival sideshows. These mummies, made by combining parts from monkeys, cats, fish, and other creatures, were crafted to look authentic, and some even made their way overseas. In Japan, they are preserved in temples, shrines, and museums.

COLUMN

この本に出てきた
妖怪の主な伝承地

The Major Legendary Regions Where the Yokai in This Book Appeared

❶ 悪路王 [*Akuro-ō*] (P.13)
❷ 安達原の鬼婆
   [The *Oni-baba* of Adachigahara] (P.27)
❸ 玉藻前 [*Tamamo no Mae*] (P.83)
❹ 化け地蔵 [*Bake-jizō*] (P.144)
❺ 百々目鬼 [*Dodomeki*] (P.16)
❻ 分福茶釜 [*Bunbuku Chagama*] (P.84)
❼ お岩 [*Oiwa*] (P.32)
❽ 雪女 [*Yuki-onna*] (P.69)
❾ 鬼女紅葉 [*Kijo-Momiji*] (P.24)

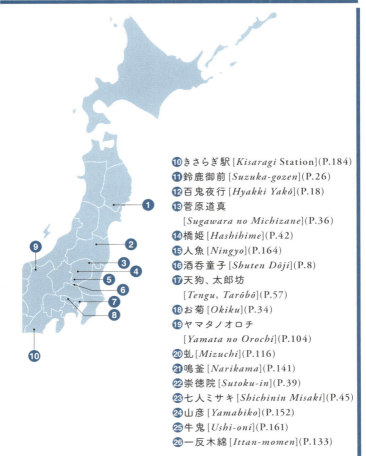

- ⑩ きさらぎ駅 [*Kisaragi* Station](P.184)
- ⑪ 鈴鹿御前 [*Suzuka-gozen*](P.26)
- ⑫ 百鬼夜行 [*Hyakki Yakō*](P.18)
- ⑬ 菅原道真 [*Sugawara no Michizane*](P.36)
- ⑭ 橋姫 [*Hashihime*](P.42)
- ⑮ 人魚 [*Ningyo*](P.164)
- ⑯ 酒呑童子 [*Shuten Dōji*](P.8)
- ⑰ 天狗、太郎坊 [*Tengu, Tarōbō*](P.57)
- ⑱ お菊 [*Okiku*](P.34)
- ⑲ ヤマタノオロチ [*Yamata no Orochi*](P.104)
- ⑳ 虯 [*Mizuchi*](P.116)
- ㉑ 鳴釜 [*Narikama*](P.141)
- ㉒ 崇徳院 [*Sutoku-in*](P.39)
- ㉓ 七人ミサキ [*Shichinin Misaki*](P.45)
- ㉔ 山彦 [*Yamabiko*](P.152)
- ㉕ 牛鬼 [*Ushi-oni*](P.161)
- ㉖ 一反木綿 [*Ittan-momen*](P.133)

おわりに

日本には古代からたくさんの妖怪が生まれては消え去っていきました。現在、妖怪はポップカルチャーの領域で生み出されるばかりでなく、各地で観光資源として見直されています。鳥取県境港市には日本を代表する妖怪漫画家水木しげるの記念館がありますが、駅からそこに至る約800mの道を水木ロードといって、妖怪像がたくさん並んでおり、まさに当地は妖怪のメッカといえましょう。

また各地に伝わる妖怪伝承にちなむ菓子や玩具、人形などのみやげ物はもちろん、京都市一条通の妖怪仮装行列や岩手県遠野市の河童釣りの体験、栃木県の殺生石のPROJECT9bによるデジタル技術を駆使した試みなど妖怪にまつわるイベントや娯楽も数知れずあります。

本書ではなるべく地域と繋がりのある妖怪を紹介しました。これを手がかりに訪れた先々で新たな妖怪との出会いがあることを願います。

Afterword

Throughout Japan's history, many yokai have appeared and disappeared. Today, yokai are not only being created in the realm of pop culture but also being rediscovered as tourist attractions in various regions.

For example, in Sakaiminato City, Tottori Prefecture, there is a memorial museum dedicated to *Shigeru Mizuki*, one of Japan's most prominent yokai manga artists. The approximately 800-meter road from the station to the museum is called Mizuki Road and is lined with numerous yokai statues. This area can truly be called the Mecca of yokai.

Additionally, there are various yokai -related souvenirs such as sweets, toys, and dolls inspired by regional yokai legends. Events and attractions include the yokai costume parade on Ichijō Street in Kyoto Prefecture, *kappa* fishing experiences in Tōno City, Iwate Prefecture, and cutting-edge digital initiatives like those by PROJECT9b at *Sesshō-seki* (the Killing Stone) in Tochigi Prefecture.

In this book, we tried to introduce yokai that have connections to specific regions. We hope that this serves as a guide, and that you will have the opportunity to encounter new yokai during your travels.

監修者　伊藤慎吾（ITO Shingo）
弘前学院大学教授。日本の妖怪文化を中心に、物語文学やキャラクター文化について研究している。人間以外のキャラクターについて研究報告や情報提供、談話をする「異類の会」(https://irui.zoku-sei.com/) を主宰。著書に『「もしも？」の図鑑 ドラゴンの飼い方』（実業之日本社）『南方熊楠と日本文学』（勉誠出版）『擬人化と異類合戦の文芸史』（三弥井書店）などがある。

本書に関するお問い合わせは、書名・発行日・該当ページを明記の上、下記のいずれかの方法にてお送りください。電話でのお問い合わせはお受けしておりません。
・ナツメ社 web サイトの問い合わせフォーム
　https://www.natsume.co.jp/contact
・FAX（03-3291-1305）
・郵送（下記、ナツメ出版企画株式会社宛て）
なお、回答までに日にちをいただく場合があります。正誤のお問い合わせ以外の書籍内容に関する解説・個別の相談は行っておりません。あらかじめご了承ください。

ナツメ社Webサイト
https://www.natsume.co.jp
書籍の最新情報（正誤情報を含む）は
ナツメ社Webサイトをご覧ください。

YOKAI
Japanese Mysterious Monsters and Phenomena

2025 年 5 月 7 日　初版発行

監修者	伊藤慎吾（いとうしんご）	Ito Shingo, 2025
発行者	田村正隆	
発行所	株式会社ナツメ社 東京都千代田区神田神保町 1-52 ナツメ社ビル 1F（〒 101-0051） 電話 03-3291-1257（代表）　FAX 03-3291-5761 振替 00130-1-58661	
制　作	ナツメ出版企画株式会社 東京都千代田区神田神保町 1-52 ナツメ社ビル 3F（〒 101-0051） 電話 03-3295-3921（代表）	
印刷所	ラン印刷社	

ISBN978-4-8163-7715-0　　　　　　　　　　　　　　　　　　Printed in Japan
〈定価はカバーに表示してあります〉〈乱丁・落丁本はお取り替えします〉
本書の一部または全部を著作権法で定められている範囲を超え、ナツメ出版企画株式会社に無断で複写、複製、転載、データファイル化することを禁じます。